LASSETER'S
LAST RIDE

ETT IMPRINT
PO Box R1906
Royal Exchange NSW 1225 Australia

First published by Angus & Robertson Publishers 1931. Reprinted 1931 (three), 1932 (seven), 1933 (three), 1934 (two), 1935, 1936 (two), 1937 (two), 1938 (two), 1939 (three), 1941, 1942, 1943, 1945, 1947, 1948, 1950, 1951, 1952, 1953, 1959, 1963 (two), 1969, 1973 (three), 1980, 1991.
Published by ETT Imprint in 2020. Reprinted 2022.
Published in London by Jonathan Cape in 1936. Reprinted 1937.
First electronic edition published by ETT Imprint in 2017.

© Idriess Enterprises Pty Ltd, 2017, 2020.

ISBN   978-1-922384-71-3   (pbk)
ISBN   978-1-922384-72-0   (ebk)

LASSETER'S
LAST RIDE

An Epic of Central Australian Gold
Discovery

Ion Idriess

ETT IMPRINT
Exile Bay

CONTENTS

1. LASSETER'S STORY

He was a little man, but you looked at him twice – he was so short, so broad, his blue eyes so determined. He walked into the office of the Australian Workers Union in Macdonell House, Pitt Street, Sydney. In that busy office he had to wait his turn among a crowd of shearers who were signing on for work in distant sheds. But Lasseter was used to waiting: he had waited years. Eventually he cornered John Bailey in his office. The President submitted good-humouredly. A patient man, he hears many a "tale" in that office, periodically visited by roaming men. This morning Bailey listened to an unusual story.

Lasseter had found a gold reef; the yellow stuff was in it thick as plums in a pudding. It lay away out in Central Australia, near the Western Australian border, right on the desert fringe. He had been prospecting for rubies in the MacDonnell Ranges, had lost himself, and found the reef. Afterwards, he got properly lost in the desert; his horses perished one by one. An Afghan camel driver found him raving with thirst and clutching a bag of gold specimens, and carried him to the surveying camp on the Western Australian Stock Route. Surveyor Harding nursed him back to life; then suggested that they both return to the reef. But the desert had put the fear of death into Lasseter for the time being.

Three years later he and Harding went out and re-located the reef. On returning to Carnarvon they were dismayed to find their watches one hour and fifteen minutes behind Carnarvon time. This meant that if their time had been incorrect when they took bearings of the reef, their location was incorrect also.

Westralia was in the fever of a great gold boom. Gold was "everywhere" – to be had practically for the digging up. No moneyed men had time or inclination to equip an expedition to work a gold reef in far-away Centralia. Lasseter joined the fevered throng to one of the new gold rushes. Harding died. Years passed and the goldfields waned. In 1916 the Western Australian Government sent out several camel expeditions to locate Lasseter's reef. The expeditions suffered casualties at the hands of the blacks and were forced to return.

Since then, Lasseter had tried in vain to get a thoroughly equipped expedition to search for his reef. He wanted Bailey to organize such an expedition now. It was not merely to re-find a gold reef; it was to open up a new goldfield and develop a new State. A great country was out there. Certainly there was desert, but a great area was not desert at all.

That, in short, was Lasseter's story. Bailey listened quietly. The man before him was obviously sincere. His heart was in his story, even though he spoke with a curious defiance, due probably to many disappointing interviews. Bailey promised nothing, but said he would investigate the strange story. He did, and was surprised. Harding's documents were searched for, and found pigeon-holed in government offices. Long-forgotten reports in Western and South Australian Mining Departments were fossicked out. From unexpected sources, too, the nuggety man's story in many particulars was substantiated.

John Bailey delved deeper. He found that some of the foremost geologists in Australia had recorded their belief that through Centralia runs a continuation of the famous Kalgoorlie ore belt. These experienced scientists prophesied that the next great goldfield would be found in the country of Lasseter's story. Any expedition going through this unexplored country would, possibly, locate a mineral field quite apart from the little man's find. A new goldfield would solve Australia's financial crisis. Then there was the individual point of view. Gold is the one commodity the value of which had risen. In good times worth £4 per ounce, it was now, with the exchange and bonus, worth nearer £5. Money put into an attempt to locate a goldfield would have a better chance of dividends than many a commercial undertaking of today.

Prominent people became interested, and £5,000 was raised within a few hours to float a company. The company was named the "Central Australian Gold Exploration Coy Ltd." One outstanding feature was that all work in connection with the formation and administration of the company was to be on a purely honorary basis. The directors and the secretary, Mr E. H. Bailey, would receive no remuneration for services rendered.

The objects of the company were to locate Lasseter's reef, to prospect for any new mineral belt, and to look for new country suitable for grazing purposes. A ground-party travelling per truck was to be sent out, with an aeroplane to co-operate. The 'plane was to keep the ground-party in touch with civilization and to search ahead of the party, locating water and a practicable route for the truck. A six-wheeled, two and a half ton Thornycroft truck, especially designed and built for trackless desert exploration, was supplied for six months, free of charge; to the company by the Thornycroft people as Britain's contribution to the expedition. This truck was secured as the result of negotiations carried through by Mr Charles Lexius-Burlington interesting Mr A. G. Hebblewhite, Thornycroft's Australian manager. It was a sister to the lorry used in the search for the bodies of the late Lieutenant Keith Anderson and his mechanic, Hitchcock. Major de Havilland's famous 'plane Black Hawk II was bought to co-operate between the prospecting ground-party and their base of supplies. The Black Hawk was renamed the Golden Quest. The Atlantic Union Oil Co. donated 600 gallons of petrol, and the benefit of their extensive free transport, and the State Government granted free transport, for the lorry, stores and men of the ground-party. The Silverton Tramway Co. were unstinting in their help.

Lasseter (front) and Blakeley (second right).

The prospecting party chosen were Fred Blakeley, leader; Harry Lasseter, guide; George Sutherland, prospector and miner; Phillip Taylor, engineer; Captain Blakiston-Houston, explorer; and E. H. Coote, pilot.

The personnel of the expedition was practically duplicated, each man, with the exception of Lasseter, being capable of undertaking another man's work. This was the best equipped prospecting expedition that ever started out in Australia. There was even a wireless transmitting and receiving set, with arrangements made through the Postmaster General for the reception of messages at Wyndham. Unfortunately, the party was detained in Sydney a considerable time after the date arranged for leaving. This meant a big difference to Blakiston-Houston, A.D.C. to Lord Stonehaven, who was due to return to his duties upon a specified date.

The Thornycroft was entrained to Broken Hill. From there Lasseter drove it overland to Quorn, on the North to South railway, where Blakeley and Sutherland linked up for Alice Springs. Meanwhile, Pilot Coote was farewelled at Mascot, and picking up Taylor at Parkes, set off on his long flight overland.

The picturesque little township of Alice Springs nestles upon a plain, with its white houses half hidden by shady trees. Each home has its well of clear water at a depth rarely exceeding twenty-five feet. Yet that country was once described as "waterless." The abrupt wall of the MacDonnell Ranges rises in the background. Alice Springs has built itself an aerodrome in anticipation of the times when it may be Australia's "halfway aviation house" to the East. At present the town is the centre of lonely cattle stations, thousands of square miles in extent. A big country, with big men and big jobs! The Government Resident controls a country the size of half a dozen European kingdoms. Sergeant Lovegrove's police district covers 236,000 square miles. The A.I.M. Sisters think a five-hundred-mile trip by car, horse, camel, or donkey team, to help a sick man, all in the day's routine. Father Long's little parish is larger than Ireland. The women of that country are wonderful.

With the arrival of the expedition excitement ran high, fanned by reports of other well-equipped expeditions coming from south and west, also searching for Lasseter's reef. Five days later, Captain Blakiston-Houston arrived, and an hour later a shout arose as the Golden Quest came droning from the sky. Alice Springs has seen many a horse and camel prospecting expedition start out into the unknown, but never an expedition like this.

The new arrivals were quickly informed that a motor truck expedition, under Michael Terry, had set out the previous week, presumably in search of the reef. Another big expedition was *en route* from Western Australia. Old papers, maps, and records had been found in Perth. Men had now a fair idea as to the location of the reef. Experienced bushmen were going to follow on the tracks of every party. And so on.

"Let them all come – if they can!" smiled Lasseter, grimly.

For the next few days the party took off their coats and got busy, cheered by the sight of the Governor's aide-de-camp in his shirt-sleeves lugging heavy cases from the railway yards to the truck. Believing speed to be doubly important now, Blakeley engaged the services of an auxiliary truck with Fred Colson, a cheerful Aussie bushman, with a reputation for initiative and resource as a driver. He lent his Chevrolet car to bring back from Ilbilba Captain Houston, who would soon be due to return to his duties.

Taylor, throughout the trip, had an insatiable desire for native curios. The blacks about the town soon exploited this hobby and Taylor was besieged with offers of coolamons, churingas, spears, wommeras, and boomerangs. One man even wanted to sell his wife – a luxury Taylor declined. The eager sellers could understand money, but their arithmetic was mixed.

"How much you want longa these feller spears?" inquired Taylor.

"Two pound, seventeen tchilling an' five bob!" was the unhesitating reply. No matter what the price, it always ended up in "five bob!"

During a "breather", Taylor and Sutherland were leaning over a counter of a shop, the proprietor of which deals largely in second-hand articles. A gin, dressed with simple taste in a single garment of scarlet print came in. She threw down a two-shilling piece and, with the bargain light in her eye, pointed across the counter.

"Gibbit that one!" she demanded.

The proprietor turned toward a shelf on which hung oddments of dress materials, and reached down a patched pair of boots.

"No, not that one – *that* one!" She pointed with emphasis.

The commercial man reached for a string of beads.

"No, not that one," said the lady disgustedly, "*That* one, that feller belly legging!!"

"Oh," said the storekeeper, as he reached down a pair of well-worn corsets, "why didn't you say so before?"

The Golden Quest at Alice Springs Airport.

2. WIRELESS IN THE DESERT

It was decided that the entire party should travel on in the trucks until a suitable landing-ground was located. Then Coote was to return to Alice Springs and fly back with the *Golden Quest*, at present under canvas at the aerodrome two miles south of the town. So Alice Springs turned out one morning to see the 'plane settle gracefully in the main street of their town. All hands helped to wheel it to the Government Residency, where it was housed snugly and in dignity. That was for safety. The aerodrome is open to the world, and nightly the 'plane had been noisily inspected by wandering horses, camels, goats, and donkeys, which would persist in nosing, biting, horning and kicking this new bird. Worse still, the fowls chose it for a roost. The animal kingdom is by no means friendly to an interloper.

The trucks were loaded scientifically. Houston was the most cheerful worker, even when a case of tinned meat fell on his foot. Stripped for labour, tall and wiry, with a heavy case on his shoulder, he looked the typical Queensland stockman rather than a noble lord's A.D.C.

Six hundred gallons of petrol, a hundred gallons of water, and two tons of provisions and equipment were loaded. Colson's auxiliary Chevrolet carried two tons of petrol. All Alice Springs turned out to give the modern cavalcade a rousing farewell. And on 21July, 1930, speeded by shouts of goodwill, the party departed to mark a new era in Australian prospecting and exploration.

Across good travelling country they made forty-three miles that afternoon, and were turning in for the night when Carrington, the Government Resident, and Constable Turnbull rode into camp. They had followed the tracks all that distance to deliver a telegram. It was a wireless code by which Blakeley had to keep in touch with his principals in Sydney.

With the great wall of the MacDonnell Ranges running parallel in the west, the party pushed cheerfully on across plains of stunted mulga and spinifex. On the second day they camped at Hamilton Downs station dam, eighty miles west of Alice Springs.

The sheet of water was covered with waterfowl, the air a-whirr with gay-plumaged parrots, flocks of topknot and bronze-wing pigeons, while zebra finches and budgerigars swept to the water in humming clouds of colour.

Archie Giles, son of the explorer, had a camp "somewhere about".

Blakeley, after a seven-mile walk, located him in a creek tucked away in the MacDonnell Ranges. Giles, nearly as broad as he is long, sixty years of age, and tough as whip-cord, is a fine type of pioneer. His happy, laughing disposition was very manifest now. After a strenuous lifetime he had just lost three thousand head of his breeding cows. "But it's a fine country," he said, dreamily, as he gazed over hill and plain; "the cattle will breed up again." He had split the comparatively few that were left into two mobs, with black stockmen shepherding them.

Giles lent his most intelligent black boy, "Micky", to Blakeley. Micky was a plump aboriginal, with inquiring eyes and a smile like that of a chewing-gum queen. He was not too keen on the party, but after inspecting their tucker supply he became quite gracious. Born in this locality, Micky knew the waterholes; but was scared of travelling out of his own "country". "Myall blackfellow spear a man quick!" he explained. The three men returned to Blakeley's camp on camels.

The party filled up the spare water tanks at the dam: the muddy yellow water could at least be used for slopping. Water *is* water in that country, and the rule was to fill the tanks at every opportunity.

Next morning the party left all semblance of a track, travelling by compass for Ilbilba, which was to be their base. From Ilbilba they would set out to locate the reef. This now famous base has been a native camping-ground from time immemorial, because of a permanent native well there. It had been located and used as a base and 'drome by the Mackay Aerial Expedition a few months previously, and its position and the fact of a 'drome having been cleared would make it an ideal base for Blakeley's party.

As they travelled on, mountain ranges closed on either side, rising sheer when the trucks were driven along the foothills. The uplift of the earth in bygone tremors had piled these barriers in masses of layered rock, and the weathering of ages had given them most unusual forms. As the miles sped by sand-ridges appeared, running parallel between the ranges.

"I'm blest if that's not a rabbit-warren," cried Coote, as he pointed to a huge burrow. It was. But the party saw only one rabbit in three hundred miles; the recent big drought had wiped them out.

The trucks lumbered on, grinding their way up the valleys, rumbling over rock, whining through sand, crunching down mulga sapling and desert shrub, and whispering over tufted spinifex, day after day under a cloudless sky.

Geologists say Central Australia is one of the oldest regions above water. Who knows but in reality it may have been the cradle of the human race! In numbers of the dried up watercourses, that once were great rivers, are petrified bones of long-extinct animals, legs and thighs that resemble slabs of ironstone. On the plains are logs of ironstone, really the petrified remains of once vast forests.

Lasseter loading the 6-wheeled Thornycroft. The Thornycroft was especially designed for off-road desert exploration

Far across the Westralian border the mountains end abruptly at the true Australian desert – sandy wastes upon which not even a camel could live. But a large part of the "dead heart" of Australia is really what is termed the "desert fringe" – areas of country upon which nutritive pastures spring up with the rains: a vast slice of our country, in many places not yet trodden by white man.

Micky, the "civilized" black boy, joined in the spirit of the party once he was assured of good and plentiful tucker. Those wondrous machines, to him, clanked with the mysteries of Aladdin's cave. The six wheels of the Thornycroft, in particular, intrigued him.

"All a same plurry sentypede," he mused, adding, "legs belonga him go round. Him make noise all a same mad bull camel. Him drink water all a same too," he declared, as he watched them pouring in the petrol. "Him thirsty cow!"

Taylor blew a blast on the horn and Micky jumped three feet, to join shakily in the laughter while staring askance at the truck.

"What you looking for now, Micky?" asked Blakeley. "Him got wild horse longa belly?" inquired Micky. "Brumby horse sing out all a same longa that one!"

Micky listened while Blakeley explained the "big feller bird" that was to fly to them, and of a man who would step out of its "belly". Micky tried hard to understand, then delight dawned on his rugged black face.

"This plurry big feller," nodding admiringly at the truck, "him husband belong big feller bird! White man piccanin belonga him!"

To save explanation, they let Micky have his own interpretation. Next he went and stuck his nose under the exhaust pipe, to "smell him breath belonga him". Micky could never get the word tractor or truck, but pronounced "motor-car", perfectly. Henceforth the Thornycroft was "motor-car" to him. In similar hazy fashion he guided them to the infrequent waterholes.

"Where him water?" asked Blakeley, as the party stared into the gloom of a rapidly approaching night.

"Jus' up there! longa that sthone," and Micky nodded cheerfully towards a range two miles away.

Mick always called any range of mountains a "sthone". They left the trucks in charge of Sutherland, walked to the hills, then clambered seven hundred feet up along a brumby-pad and found the water to be a spring-filled rock-hole, smelling of animal visitors. Clambering down those slippery rocks in the dark, hugging nine-gallon drums of water, gave them a gnawing appetite for supper.

Meanwhile, Sutherland had baked a damper, put the billy warming by the fire, and beside it the washing up billy filled with the milky yellow water from Hamilton Dam. Coote grabbed his plate of meat and damper, hungrily set to, and reached for the tea billy. So did Houston, and waded into his meal. He enjoyed his first cup of tea immensely. At the second he remarked:

"This tea tastes sort of fishy."

"What's wrong with it?" smiled Sutherland. "There's plenty of cow in it, isn't there?"

"Now I come to think of it," said Houston, as he thoughtfully sipped the tea, "there's too much damn cow in it! I've been sugaring and milking this beastly slopping-up water, and you never said a word!"

Lasseter roared laughing, but he never let on that he too had mixed his drinks.

"Plenty cow swim longa that water," volunteered Micky. "He wash him there; he stay longa dam all day; sometimes he sleep!"

"You needn't rub it in," spat Houston, disgustedly.

Late next afternoon a flat-topped range like a wall of rock completely blocked their way. It meant an earlier camp than was expected until a way was found round the range.

"Where the hell *is* this water?" demanded Blakeley.

Micky had sworn he could locate yet another spring today. Unconcernedly, he looked towards a range five miles distant. "Over there," he nodded, "longa that sthone!" He thought machines that could break through timber, climb over rocks, lumber down into creeks and up out again could surely climb mountains. The party found that the rougher the country the greater the consumption of water. On the afternoon of the following day it became increasingly clear that Micky's sense of locality was waning.

"Me think him water this way!" he would nod seriously. Then, after a fruitless search, "No, him this way." Micky had reached the boundary of his "country". Henceforth he was to be a willing worker but almost useless so far as a guide to water was concerned. They camped in the farflung shadows cast by mighty rocks.

Colson set out to try and locate a large creek called the Dashwood, while Blakeley walked up along a likely looking gorge. Spreading green trees grew there, and a well-trodden brumby-pad seemed to lead to water. From far up the gorge came the melodious note of a bell-bird. Darkness fell and Blakeley abandoned the quest for the night. At the camp, Taylor had lashed the spotlight to a sapling tied above the Thornycroft as a guide to Colson.

Late that night Micky suddenly exclaimed: "Me hear him; Fred find him water alright." They stood up around the fire listening to the swishing of bushes, then Colson's cheery voice telling he had located a soak.

"How did you know Fred find him water?" asked Blakeley of Micky.

"Feet belong him speak longa me!" answered Micky, as if surprised that the men, too, could not hear feet "talking".

Next morning they pressed on to the soak. It was only a scooped-out hole in the sand in a large dry creek where brumbies had been pawing for water. They camped, dug a well and logged it up, and soon there was a plentiful supply. Though this country is undoubtedly dry, it is not so dry as its reputation. Numbers of dry creeks contain "soak" water just a few feet below the surface, as the wild animals well know. They use nose, claw and hoof to find it. Artesian bores would probably reach lakes of water underneath.

To commemorate the way he could handle a pick and shovel, this soak was christened "Houston's Soak". The recipient accepted the honour gracefully.

Taylor was busy for the next few days with the oxy-acetylene plant welding minor repairs. The welding outfit proved of inestimable benefit to the party. Future expeditions using mechanized transport may thereby take a hint. Further, the services of a first-class engineer and mechanic, such as Taylor proved himself to be, are invaluable. He kept the motor and flying-machines of the expedition always up to their mechanical work.

At this soak Taylor shot their first 'roo. 'Roo-tail soup was a welcome addition to the bill of fare. Micky was in ecstasy; for this unfortunate 'roo carried a baby in its pouch. Mick, tenaciously gripping the baby, explained that this food was a delicacy, "taboo" to all the young men of his tribe. Only the old men were allowed to eat it. And now this luxury that he had expected to enjoy only in his crafty old age was in his hands. Micky cooked his stolen delight on a little fire away by himself.

The nights were very cold. Each man had a camp stretcher which turned into a freezer when the cool air got under it. This taught each would-be sleeper to fill a bag with grass as a mattress.

Next morning at packing-up Houston inquired of Blakeley: "What about this blooming 'roo?"

"Oh, shove it in a bag," answered Blakeley, absently, as he regulated the packing of the truck. That was no small job each morning! The tucker-box and camping gear were always stacked in a handy position. Everything must be securely lashed. They pushed on, Micky full of pride in that he had learnt to sit on the tail of the truck without falling off. While surging up a gully bank the truck jolted over a log and Micky landed, whoof! on his bingy.

That night, after the evening smoke-oh, the party turned in healthily tired. It was very cold leaving the camp fire. Sutherland, his long spare form trying to sink into the narrow stretcher, could not get comfortable. He twisted and turned and shivered and grumbled as first his bare feet and then his head poked out of the blankets. He could not work into a cosy position; his bed seemed all clammy bumps. At last he stepped out into the cold, grumbling; "I feel I'm lying on a frozen corpse." He reached his arm down into the mattress, then roared – "who the hell shoved half a kangaroo into my bag?"

"Oh," chuckled a smothered voice, "I did; so sorry!"

3. THE KADITCHA

The next few days were through country in which the party constantly had to mat the truck's wheels across soft sand, dig cuttings down steep embankments, and swing the axe on timber.

Sighing, as from a hard day's work well and truly done, the party sat down to tea. Micky, who always dined a little aside, edged up to Sutherland, his eyes and mouth smiling in anticipation. Sutherland cut him a hunk of damper, sliced off a lump of cheese, of which Micky had grown very fond, and gave him a helping of meat.

"Oh, by the way, Micky, where's your 'roo?" the cook inquired.

"Him tinkin," grinned Micky as he walked away chewing. "Me trow him away. Tchese more better."

"Cheese smell, too," said Blakeley.

"Yeh!" answered Micky, "but me eatem that feller smell."

"This tea is damn weak," remarked Coote, disparagingly. "Tastes like boarding-house tea to me; now you taste it and now you don't!"

"Why, the leaves aren't settled!" exclaimed Lasseter as he peered into the billy. "Who boiled it?"

"Phil did," smiled Sutherland, accusingly. "Why didn't you boil the tea, Phil?"

"I made the water as hot as we'll drink it," answered Taylor indignantly. "What more do you want!" But the party unanimously decided that Phil Taylor was no cook.

Next day a broad, tree-shaded creek stretched before them, showing a shimmering expanse of fine white sand. The Thornycroft poised a moment on the steep bank; then, as her nose lurched downward, the men gripped their seats while Micky took no chances on the back. With a grinding of brakes the big vehicle lurched down, then ploughed deep into the sand that showered hissing from the spinning wheels.

"All hands to the mats!" shouted Blakeley.

"Aye, aye, sir!" cried the crew, as they leaped off and pulled out fifty-foot strips of coconut fibre matting, eighteen inches wide. These strips were laid down in front of the trucks and gave the wheels a moderately firm purchase. It took a steady hand at the steering-wheel, though, to keep the truck wheels on the narrow strips and still dodge stones, ruts and logs. There was a knack, too, for the crew to learn in holding the strips so that they were not pulled in all askew under the gripping tyres. That order "All hands to the mats!" grew monotonous over every sandy stage of the journey. As the country became rougher, Blakeley would walk far ahead of the truck, seeking a clearer path amongst the timber and round sandhills, while trying to dodge creeks and still keep on a compass course for Ilbilba.

Several days later an unmapped creek (a river in ages past) effectually blocked their way. All hands jumped out and got busy digging a cutting down into the creek and a larger one up the opposite bank. A hundred yards of the creek-bed had to be corduroyed (a road of logs made across it) – a stiff road-gang job.

Taylor yelled "Hurrah!" as the big Thornycroft rumbled down the cutting and crunched on to the corduroy, lurching over the logs and grinding them into the sand to the crackling of bush and squashing of bark. Taylor was nippy at the steering-wheel and gears in negotiating the causeway of bucking logs. As she came to the western bank her nose rose up and she coughed skyward like a lumbersome tank. Slowly her tail came up level, and Blakeley sighed in relief.

But the auxiliary truck could not do it. She stripped a pinion. A hasty council was held. Time would be needed for repairs; and Houston was due to return to his duties shortly. Portion of this creek was very lightly timbered; if cleared it would make a serviceable landing-ground. Here was a chance to take Houston back and return with the 'plane. It was decided that Colson should return to Alice Springs with Houston and Coote, while the airman and Colson would return later in the 'plane. Meanwhile, Taylor would repair the auxiliary truck while the others cleared a landing-ground.

Said Houston, as he wiped the sweat from his noble brow, "If we've done nothing else we've certainly made a road." And he retired to the shade of a tree to mend his trousers.

A regretful party said good-bye to Houston. His capability and unfailing cheeriness had made him very much liked.

"He's a damn good bushman gone to waste," said Sutherland, regretfully, as they watched the Chevrolet disappear through the bush.

"Him plurry white man!" voted Micky.

The party had the luck to locate a splendid forty-thousand-gallon-a-day spring up in the range not far from the creek. The spring was a watering place for birds; while wild horse, wallaby, euro, and dingo tracks showed how popular this cool rock-hole was with the other denizens of the wild. It was the last water the party saw until they arrived at Ilbilba.

The water question solved, the men got busy with the aerodrome. After some days' strenuous work, a very fair little landing-ground had been cleared when a rapidly approaching hum attracted anxious eyes upwards, while Coote circled low over the trees, then landed the 'plane like a gracefully swooping bird. All hurried forward to congratulate him. The handling of the *Golden Quest* might mean a lot towards the future success of the expedition. Colson was glad to step on firm ground; the flight had been "bumpier" than a trip at sea. The 'plane did the two hundred and forty miles in two and a half hours – the trucks had taken nine days.

Micky approved of the 'plane. His smile expressed more than words. With eyes bulging like onions he walked round and round the 'plane, peering under it, peeping into the cockpit, all the while on tiptoes, ready to run. He clucked his admiration like an old hen. The evening meal was hardly powerful enough to drag him from the wonder. The propeller blades particularly took his fancy. As he stroked them with reverent hands he said:

"By cri', good feller boomerang this one." Micky was not satisfied until Blakeley promised him a ride "sometime."

Taylor overhauled the 'plane. Then it was covered, securely tied down, and left until called for at "Taylor's Creek."

At this creek Micky, with toes, hands and tomahawk, climbed a sixty-foot tree, and set aerial wires. The party was looking forward to seeing Mick's first reception of wireless. They tested the machines, and found they could receive but not transmit. Magnetic iron sands in the ground may have been responsible. They put the earphones on Micky. Seated on a box, he submitted with a grin, anticipating anything might happen. Something did. Statics! Micky bolted. When they caught him they held him down, patting him as they would a horse. They hung on until he got the music which "soothes the savage beast." The glare faded from his eyes; his breast heaved less riotously; the frightened gash that was his mouth expanded into a grin that spread from ear to ear; his eyes grew normal, then sparkled.

Micky was "set"; he was a wireless enthusiast. He sat erect, with teeth gleaming, listening to the band. They could almost see down his throat. The band faded out. When the jazz orchestra entertained Micky, his two big toes stood to attention, then got the jerks.

"What you think longa that feller?" inquired Blakeley.

"By cri'," grinned Micky, "me think him plurry big feller corroboree that one! Plurry big one altogether!"

One wonders how that particular orchestra would have taken the compliment. Leaping from the box, Micky peered all round the wireless machine, listening, searching, trying to locate the man who was making the music.

"Him plurry funny feller," he chuckled regretfully. "Maybe I catch him sometime; him altogether too funny!" Thereafter, throughout the trip, at every gumtree they came to, Micky wanted to get out and set the aerial wires.

Cheerfully the party pressed on. Life was full of pep. They were on the search for gold, and were now in new country. Soon they would enter country never trodden by white men. Who could tell what lay before them?

The Thornycroft would be plugging along to a continual grinding in low gear, ploughing over sand, rumbling across gullies, dodging heavy timber to the crackling of dead sticks and snapping of saplings, when suddenly would come a break of clear going through the bush ahead. Taylor, with "Hurrah! Up and at 'em boys," would lift her into high gear, and the big lorry would go lumbering through the mulga with the crew bawling –

Sailing up the Clyde, sailing up the Clyde,
Back to Bonnie Scotland where the old folks bide.

Micky, clinging to the tail of the truck, would yell appreciation.

Blakeley was absorbed with his own particular job. He wanted to get the party and trucks to Ilbilba as quickly as possible. He knew that if Lasseter did not pick up his landmarks on the first trip out from Ilbilba then much time would have already been lost and money wasted. Thoughtfully he plodded on day after day ahead of the truck. Short, powerfully built, somewhat slow of speech, with clean-cut features, not so ready, perhaps, as the other members of the party to break into a laugh – his was the responsibility.

Sutherland was interested in the rocks. He would test with knapping hammer any likely formation they met, seeking a clue to the presence of gold. He was the sly humorist. A six-foot slab of typical bushman, his weather-beaten face never lacked its smile. He had the knack of turning breakfast into a laugh when on odd mornings any member of the party would awake with "liver." And he liked animals and birds and insects.

Colson, the bushman, proved a first-rate worker; tireless and always cheery. His work was cut out from sunset till dark, and sometimes later.

Taylor, almost every evening, was busy with minor repairs. Of medium height, and thin build, he just showed the stoop of many a man used for years to bending over machines. He was the typical engineer who could lose himself in a machine. He sang with his machines when he got them going well. He was always quiet when they were crotchety; but immediately the machine began to hum Taylor began to sing.

Coote was a young fellow bubbling over with enthusiasm, anxious for his job in the *Golden Quest* to begin.

Lasseter was cheerful and reserved in turns. His determined face did not belie the nature of the man within. An unusual man in several ways. One of his dreams was the Harbour Bridge. Long ago he had drawn plans for such a bridge, and those plans have been pronounced by competent engineers perfect down to the last rivet. Highly educated men with whom he came in contact have expressed their surprise at his knowledge of unusual subjects, never suggested by the man's everyday talk. His mates on this expedition found him a good camp-mate, but liable to be impatient at even unavoidable delay, and headstrong over difficulties. They had an idea, too, that though the finding of the reef occupied his mind, his ultimate object embraced something greater. As a matter of fact, at this time a subdued excitement boiled within Lasseter, as day by day every forward lurch of the trucks brought him a little nearer his lifetime's desire.

Camped in a dry creek, one morning, Taylor knelt down and examined the sand. "Here's that dingo again," he exclaimed. "You'd almost think it is the same one following us from camp to camp. Enough to give a man the creeps! Look how its tracks have sneaked right up to my bunk. It must have sniffed me while I slept."

"They say dingoes like English hams," drawled Sutherland.

"Shows their good taste," retaliated Taylor. "Here, Micky, come look longa these tracks. See which way he go."

But Micky was comfortably engaged boiling the billy. "Me think him that dingo plurry two-leg dingo," he said, with a sly glance at Sutherland.

Sutherland had to laugh – he was an expert at making dingo tracks with his hand.

The Derwent held them up for two hours before they could find a crossing over the stones. They had time to admire the sunset flooding the battlements of Haasts Bluff with soft light. Later, the Thornycroft lumbered into a sea of grey-green mulga, apparently impenetrable: no openings, no channels of lightly timbered country along which the trucks could dodge. For sixty miles they toiled with the axe. By compass bearing they cut a lane like a broad band of sunlight running through the forest.

Utterly tired at nights, they lay smoking, gazing up at the brilliant stars. Lasseter, however, did not smoke; he talked with the others until there came that quiet hush wherein men, busy with their thoughts, or to hide thoughts, only speak in monosyllables. Then he would retire within himself and dream. There was a pitch darkness around them that made the sky above a visible blue band studded with diamonds; and a silence made more intense by the stealthy crackling of leaves as if some nocturnal animal were prowling round. As they listened, there would come the long-drawn howl of a dingo, answered by its mate from far away.

With deep thankfulness the party emerged from the mulga and scanned the horizon for Mount Tudor. They were made rather anxious by the knowledge that maps of the country were based to a great extent on guess-work and surmise. After all that timber, a sandhill, upon which was silhouetted one solitary tree, immediately attracted all eyes.

"Micky," ordered Blakeley, "you go longa that hill look-about. Maybe better feller track down long other side."

But Micky stood aghast.

"What on earth is the matter?" said Blakeley, "Have you seen a ghost? Go on, Micky," he insisted.

Micky stared appealingly.

"What for you no want to go longa that hill?" asked Blakeley sternly. "Come now, quick feller talk!"

"Kaditcha!" answered the man, almost in a whisper.

Lasseter with his truck on the C.A.G.E. expedition 1930.

4. THE TRACK TO ILBILBA

They understood then and reconnoitred the one-tree hill themselves, knowing that only main force could persuade Micky there.

"Kaditcha" is the Centralian aborigines' word of terror. It conjures up stark fear; it means a terror above ordinary physical fear. Kaditcha may be represented by a sacred emblem, by meaning in a word, a belief. Often it means to them a power capable of operating from another world, a menace unfightable, a spirit power which by malign influence can be used against man. Under certain but well-defined conditions, it is a power which influences their lives from birth to death, and, they firmly believe, after death also.

That evening, taking care not to belittle Micky's fright of a few hours before, the party sought to coax from him an explanation of this particular "Kaditcha" of the tree. Micky tried hard to avoid the subject; then, glancing fearfully into the night, he mumbled that the spirit of a powerful witch-doctor lived in that tree; the tree was sacred to him; it had grown up out of his body; the living spirit of the man had power to harm any aboriginal who desecrated that tree. No tribe would even dare to camp near it. Micky would say no more. He turned in, covering himself well with the blanket; and they had to be content with what they knew to be a very shadowy explanation.

The party yarned awhile of other experiences of blackfellows and their Kaditchas, examples of the inborn power of superstition over the minds of these natives. No matter how civilized a black boy is, no matter how many years he has lived with the whites, the Kaditcha still has power over him. Lasseter was especially interested. In the days that followed he often spoke quietly to Micky, seeking to learn all he could. He had been getting the boy to teach him the "lingo", too. A knowledge of the desert tribes' dialect might prove very useful.

A week of intensely interesting travel followed. It was an eye-opener to these Australians, this "dead heart" of their country. They certainly saw plains of arid sand. But they saw also hills and mountain ranges in green, and straw-gold, and blue, large areas of Mitchell and other grasses, and belts of timber other than mulga. The foliage of these trees makes splendid fodder in drought. Brumby and wallaby pads were fairly plentiful, pointing to the presence of water in the locality. In an occasional grove of trees birds were vocal. These patches of good country relieved the monotony of mulga and spinifex.

Crunching up through a belt of timber on to an open grassy glade, the big Thornycroft must have appeared a prehistoric monster to a brumby stallion and his mares. He faced the menace. A magnificent chestnut, he stepped out with arched neck, his red mane a glory reflecting the fury in his eyes. The mares bolted with their foals. The Thornycroft stopped, and those within it sat quiet as mice. Pawing the earth the stallion plunged forward, his body trembling with pride because he had stopped this monstrous thing. Instinct bade him circle to leeward. He smelt the truck, his head stretched out, his nostrils quivering. He screamed a shrill, whistling challenge, then wheeling galloped, with tossing head and wild whistlings after his vanished harem.

These brumbies are often magnificent animals, fathered by valuable stallions that have escaped from Centralian stations. They roam the country usually in little mobs, a stallion and his harem. As the young stallions in every mob grow to maturity, the old man turns on them with tooth and hoof, and in a screaming madness drives them from the mob. But alas, time flies, strength wanes! A husky youngster arises and thrashes the old one to his knees, leaving him torn and bleeding, often to die from a broken leg, while the younger gallops off with the harem. Sometimes an old stallion is seen, scarred by many fights, feeding all alone, sullen and morose. Sometimes two or three scarred veterans drift together, shunned by the herds, a neighing menace to any stray young stallion unwary enough to venture within their reach.

The party lumbered on up past the Lebrik Mountains, their spectacular canyon and weird peaks bathed in purple, and grey, and blue, with creamy mists at sunrise rising in clouds of bridal lace. The party often speculated as to water in those mountains. The Lebriks rise in three chains, fantastically reminiscent of the lips of a once mighty volcano. The first chain of jagged points rises abruptly a thousand feet; to the south a similar broken lip rises eighteen hundred feet; then, half a mile beyond it, the third series rises three thousand feet in towering cliffs, from which huge rock masses have thundered down on to the plain.

Filled with the desire to see what lay on the other side, the party left their trucks to climb these mountains. An unbroken wall of cliffs on the south side effectually barred their way, but they found the ascent comparatively easy from the north. Looking far away south they gazed on the most fertile land they were to see in all the trip. A spreading plain, spider-webbed by black-green streaks that were the trees of creeks, lay at their feet. Miles away there shimmered four extensive waterholes – apparently merging into a series of swamps dotted here and there with mobs of wild horses. The delight of the party was increased when they found the hills alive with euros and wallabies, the plain with kangaroo rats and emus, and bird-life busy and noisy everywhere.

As they pushed on, the sandhills made their appearance again, but added a surprise in the shape of a forest of desert oak, beautiful trees with barrels of from twenty to thirty feet of unsurpassable timber, growing upon sand.

Micky was quite bushed. He would turn to any point of the compass in describing where Mount Tudor lay. While searching for it, Colson suddenly shouted "Here we are!" But instead of gazing at the big tabletop mountain, the party stared down at the wind-blown impression of a camel-pad.

"It's the old pad Bob Buck's camels made when he took the supplies to Mackay at Ilbilba," explained Colson. "No other camels would be out here. If we can follow these tracks they'll most likely take us over negotiable ground."

The trucks lumbered off, following the sometimes quite obliterated tracks of the ships of the desert. It was fitting that in this prehistoric land modern transport should give way to the transport of the Pharaohs.

The party went on short rations. The last seventy miles had been travelled at the rate of two miles per hour. The Thornycroft had never been higher than sixth gear out of its ten gears, and the radiators had consumed an alarming quantity of water.

The first sandhill that ran straight across their line of travel was seventy feet high and four hundred yards across, of soft sand, spinifex, and shrub. The Thornycroft tackled it with a growling of gears that plunged the truck on until the gripping tyres bit deep into a showering flurry of fine sand.

"More better this motor-car grow feet all a same a camel," remarked Micky, as the crew jumped out with the mats.

With this ingenious aid they climbed the hill and lumbered down the opposite side. The trucks took two and a half hours to negotiate that first hill. A wedge-tail eagle, like a speck in the sky, may have mistaken the trucks for giant tortoises, attended by toiling ants.

For some days the old pad wound among the sandhills, apparently bearing north of west of Ilbilba. In late afternoon Blakeley gazed anxiously from a sandhill across a plain of mulga and spinifex. Sundown was clothing the land in shadows of misty colours. A large bare patch in the centre of the plain Blakeley thought might be the 'drome at Ilbilba. Gladly the party pushed on; but night had fallen when they proved the "'drome" to be a patch of soft chocolate loam covered with grass two feet high. The auxiliary truck, with two tons of petrol, bogged fast. Tired after a gruelling day, her crew climbed down with shovels to dig her out, while the Thornycroft ploughed ahead.

Suddenly arose a yell "Fire under the 'Thorny'!" There was a rush as the flames licked up. Coote and Taylor sprang from the Thornycroft. Taylor was swishing a fire extinguisher on the flames, and Coote was beating the blazing grass with a blanket, as the remainder of the party rushed up with shovelfuls of sand. It was all over in moments, but what a narrow escape! The Thornycroft with her stores and two hundred gallons of petrol, the bogged auxiliary thirty yards away loaded with two tons of petrol, and under each, dense dry grass! Had the alarm been given a moment later, the party would have had to run for their lives, and would have found themselves isolated hundreds of miles from civilization with neither water nor food.

Six shaking men stared at one another in the dark. Then they sought for the cause. The heavy going had caused overheating of the exhaust pipe; it was red-hot, while the framework of the car had stripped the heads of the grasses and ignited them.

Next morning at eight o'clock the party arrived at Ilbilba aerodrome, a clearing measuring about seven hundred yards square, the work of the Mackay expedition. Substantial bough sheds and "wings" of brushwood as breakwinds were still standing. Ilbilba itself proved to be a plain, with, on the west, a parallel mountain chain stretching north and south. The expedition was in the Ehrenberg Range country, just on the fringe of the desert. This plain was very unlike the accepted idea of desert. Stunted mulga, gums, and bloodwood grew upon it, with innumerable bushes and wild flowers among the hardy spinifex. Like the grim black ranges looking so worn, all the shrubbery showed signs of battling, but successfully battling, for existence. Each desert plant was a fighter, and had instinctively adopted its own wonderful method of holding life, even though years passed without rain.

5. THE CRASH

Here Sutherland lost his reputation. He had been voted a dabster cook: he made dampers so light that they were in danger of blowing away. "More better we eat 'em quick feller!" as Mick used, gloatingly, to advise. Sutherland had not baked one "sod" during the entire trip. Neither had the others, but then they had not tried. This day, however, Sutherland was mixing his damper while the fire was burning to good hot coals. The others were away prospecting. It was a nice sunny day, without a breath of wind. Sutherland grunted cheerfully as he punched, pounded, and kneaded that big fat dish of dough. Surprising how much damper five hungry men and an abo can eat.

Suddenly across the plain there shot toward the sky a brown devil that in a spinning column rushed straight for the cook. It caught him bending and lashed him in a vortex of wind and sand, clattering with flying dishes and billycans. He flung his arms across his face, but it spun him around, whipped up his shirt, and drumming a tarpaulin, spun shrieking across the plain.

Sutherland swore and spluttered as he scraped the sand and ashes from his eyes. His first thought was for his precious damper. One blink at the once white dough was enough. He bundled it into the camp oven, sand and all – there must have been five pounds of sand in it. As he piled the coals around the oven he thought –

"Oh, well, they've had a good spin so far, a little sand won't hurt them." Then he set out in the track of the willy-willy to find his hat.

That evening, Blakeley cut into the damper. At least, he tried to. Questioningly he lifted it up, a weighty expression on his face. "Heavy as lead!" he muttered accusingly. He shoved a sheath knife into it, put his weight on the knife, and swore when the blade gritted sand.

"It's like cutting the Pyramids!" he exploded. "What the hell have you been doing?"

All parties peered into the damper. Its inside was a dirty, greyish brown, with lumps of charcoal and other things in it.

"The man's gone dippy," declared Taylor. "He is trying to poison us!"

"If I couldn't bake a better sod than that," grinned Lasseter, "I'd fry myself!"

Blakeley hacked off a hunk and tried it on Mick. Micky accepted the test dubiously. A few weeks on good food had made him "tucker proud". He opened his cavernous mouth and crunched. Then he spat out a mouthful of sand. "All a same plurry grindstone!" The party threw the damper away.

"I'm baking yeast bread after this," declared Blakeley, and he did. Mick retrieved the damper and magnanimously gave it to "the niggers."

The party walked up towards the range to locate the soak. Easy enough for those with eyes; several native "pads" converged towards it around the spinifex. Then, too, the clumps of thin-trunked trees around the hole were covered with noisy finches and small but noisier parrots, while a flock of desert pigeons, like little blue doves, rose from the bushes with a whirr of wings. The rock-hole was about five feet in diameter and six in depth, probably fed by an underground spring. This rock-hole, the only permanent one for a hundred miles, has made Ilbilba of vast importance to a handful of native tribes for untold centuries.

It was a meeting-place, too, for other life that moved within a wide radius. If a man possessed an owl's eye at night, he would have seen strange nocturnal wanderers come to that hole to drink. The taint of animals was in and around the water. No one would begrudge them a drink, but they made their presence smelt.

After a luxurious wash, the party got busy preparing the base. A sixty-foot wireless mast was erected. Then, with the battery from the truck, they tried for three days to get in touch with civilization and also to keep the directors in distant Sydney in touch with the movements of the expedition. The failure of their wireless experiments was the first big disappointment.

From the surrounding hills were rising thin, clearly distinguishable smoke columns, showing how the stone age men far and wide were communicating the presence of the white men.

Even before the party had reached Ilbilba, Micky had apprehensively pointed out these signals. And now two of those age-old men suddenly made their appearance. Standing like statues upon a rock, with barbed spears in their hands, their hair thrown back by a grass-plaited foreheadband, they stared from hawk-like eyes down upon the whites.

Signs of peace and goodwill were made to them. Presently they stepped down and walked towards the party. They had well-proportioned bodies and a panther litheness in their step. For desert natives they were in remarkably good condition. Blakeley tried by sign language to open up a conversation. To Lasseter's disappointment, Micky was of little help. He hardly understood a word of their "lingo" and clung close to the whites, obviously afraid of these "myall" countrymen of his. The wild men, however, treated their civilized brother with disdain.

As if in recognition of the party's goodwill, presently a third appeared, the tousled heads of his lubras and piccaninnies staring from distant bushes. The newcomer carried a firestick in his hand and an ingratiating smile on his wrinkled old face. He wore a moustache, a comical pointed beard and an old felt hat!

"Rip Van Winkle come to life again," drawled Sutherland. "All dressed up and nowhere to go!"

They marvelled that he should have known white men, until in energetic pantomime he pointed to the 'drome and on his hands and knees showed how he had crept from the rocks and retrieved the wonder hat as the Mackay expedition were abandoning the ground.

"We'll give the old dog a bone," smiled Sutherland. He scraped out the pots, collecting a mixture of porridge, meat scraps, tea-leaves, custard, and stewed apple; then glanced around for something to put the mess in. Old Rip Van obligingly offered his hat. The party grinned as Sutherland filled the receptacle to the brim. But they roared when the old man put the hat on his head and unconcernedly walked off, his chest streaming with custard, his back with porridge. As he walked towards his admiring lubras, he wiped the custard from his eyes and licked his fingers. Thus did old Rip Van enjoy his first taste of civilized food!

The plans of the party now were that Colson should return to Alice Springs and bring out the remainder of the petrol and supplies, leaving Coote at Taylor's Creek to bring on the *Golden Quest*. Instructions to the pilot were to take no chances if the wind was not favourable for taking off. No anxiety would be felt by the waiting party for three days. All conditions being favourable, however, the 'plane should arrive upon the same day that it started.

Having farewelled the auxiliary truck, the party, taught by experience, set about getting the Thornycroft ready for the stern work ahead. The mudguards were removed so that the driver could easily see the narrow matting when in use; a stout sapling was lashed to the buffer as a reinforcement against the shock of tree, rock, or abrupt creek bank. All were busy; all were keenly alive with the expectation of great things.

In the late afternoon Lasseter would quietly disappear. Alone on a hill, with his back to a rock lest he be a target for a spear, he would gaze far out across the desert fringe.

Sunset is wonderful in this desert. From sunset to the drawing of night's soft, dark curtain across the sky, is twenty minutes. You can see it coming from the east, that curtain, spreading rapidly across the sky as if to catch up with the golden shadows of the sun; the fading gold in the sky turns to purple-blue, deepening into velvet-black as you watch.

Colson and Coote, having their own tracks to return upon, made quick time back to Taylor's Creek and immediately set about preparations for the flight. They cleared a longer runway of three hundred yards. Beyond that were the felled gum-trees and standing timber. Coote climbed into the cockpit, warmed up the engine, and set her roaring at the full to try out the ignition. She was running as sweetly as could be desired.

Waving a cheerful farewell, he taxied forward. She was slow to rise. The trees were getting dangerously close when the engine changed its note. The machine staggered as it took the air, fluttering badly. Coote tried desperately to right her, but he was already in amongst the trees; a dead branch snapped pistol-like against the right wing, as the pilot banked sharply, seeing too late another tree immediately to the left. He cut off the switches against fire and flung an arm over his eyes as the left wing crashed and the 'plane heeled over, poised an instant on its nose, then crashed over on its back. Colson ran to the crumpled 'plane, his heart in his mouth. Coote's head was doubled against his chest, he was bleeding profusely, the smell of petrol was in the air. Colson struggled to get the hurt man clear lest the 'plane burst into flames. He worked rapidly, carrying Coote to his truck, bathing his head, and hastily making splints for his leg. He made a rude bunk of boughs on the truck, lashed the man on, and in less than an hour was driving with all his nerve and speed on the two hundred and forty miles to Alice Springs. Thankfully he remembered the foresight of the A.I.M., those people who had built a little hospital out there in the far centre. It was a nightmare drive through the night. He did the trip in twenty-two hours, in sweating fear of tragedy.

6. THE STONE AGE MEN

Meanwhile the party at Ilbilba by midday on the second day were searching the clear blue sky. The next day they ate their meals almost in silence – listening! A buzz, growing into a hum, sent Lasseter running from the bough shed, while the others stared in pleased relief. Sutherland smiled dryly as a big golden hornet came humming into the shed. Blakeley swore when an hour later that same hornet buzzed another false alarm. Night came, but no 'plane. The men stood by to light guiding fires. It was decided to run the Thornycroft some miles back over the sandhills so as to get a good start in earliest dawn. If Coote had met with mishap in the true desert it meant a matter of time in which to save him.

In case the 'plane had only been delayed, Lasseter and Micky stood by the stores at Ilbilba.

Back along their own deep tracks, the big truck was driven, crashing through mulga, tearing over the spinifex, the brakes screaming when the lights suddenly showed a tree across the track. The mulga stakes were a dread menace, for the branches, smashed by the truck on their outward trip, were now pointing directly against them. That trip meant forty-three punctures and both sides of the screen torn out, besides hours of work and anxiety.

On the afternoon of the fifth day they gazed down on Taylor's Creek and the wrecked 'plane. On the machine was a note from Colson saying he would return from Alice Springs as soon as possible. Under the direction of Taylor, they set to work dismantling the 'plane. Their hopes of a quick trip had crashed with the *Golden Quest*.

During the Thornycroft's absence, the natives in isolated batches, came to make the white men's acquaintance. They appeared silently, standing a little way off before venturing towards the camp; then approached timidly, yet with the defiant mien of men who had the right. Built as a rule on the small side, they were of good physique, compact and wiry, with hawk's eyes. Their whole physique expressed great endurance. Each man had a front tooth knocked out; chest and shoulders were cicatrized by warrior weals, and his naked body was greased with goanna fat. Their single-barbed spear-heads were of fire-hardened wood. Lasseter learned later that some of these natives were not yet even in the stone age. During the months in which Ilbilba formed a base, however, there came into camp several tribes, apparently living away to the north-east, who understood the chipping of stone. These men wore around their waists a plaited string of human hair, in which was twisted a stone knife with a handle of fire-baked clay. The generally curved blade of the knife rested in an ingenious sheath of tea-tree bark, sewn with animal-fur thread. Lasseter, though ever on the alert, was friendly towards all visitors, constantly seeking to pick up a native word here and there, and to get an inkling of their customs and superstitions.

By degrees, women came towards the camp, mostly in pairs – shy, big-eyed, wild as desert rats, yet drawn by an insatiable curiosity. They were in good condition, as straight as an arrow. Their legs were conspicuously more shapely than the general spindle shanks of the aboriginal, and the young girls' breasts were plumply developed. Rains had broken the drought in this country and all were waxing fat on the plentiful animal and plant foods that quickly appeared.

Lasseter hid many a smile at the "dress" of these women. The majority were perfectly naked. Some, however, had picked up cast-off clothing after the Mackay expedition left camp: and these clothes, torn to shreds in fights for the wonder material, were worn proudly – not always in the right place.

The truck party away back at Taylor's Creek were heavy in sleep one quiet dawn, when Sutherland sleepily drawled, "I hear the hum of a truck!"

"So's your grandmother," mumbled Taylor, "got 'planeitis and motoritis very bad! Shut up and give the birds a chance to wake."

But breakfast was only just cooked when Colson arrived. Sutherland had heard the engine fifteen miles away. Sound carries long distances in the clear Centralian air.

"Coote's all right," said Colson cheerily; "the A.I.M. Sisters are patching him up. My truck is the next casualty. I collided with one tree too many and broke the nut off a front wheel."

While Taylor was oxy-welding the nut, the party loaded the 'plane on to the truck. Colson was to truck the 'plane to Alice Springs, where it would be trained to Adelaide for repairs. He would then return to Ilbilba with more petrol and stores.

The Thornycroft lumbered back on its return trip, its crew rather silent. Long before they reached Ilbilba Sutherland nodded towards the heavy smoke-columns rising among the hills, where Lasseter signalled by day while he waited for the 'plane. A gloomy quietness descended on the three men – almost a premonition that those would not be the last smoke-signals Lasseter would light for a 'plane that never came.

Lasseter took the news quietly. It would possibly be months now before the 'plane could return. The party would either have to do without its services as a path-finder and seeker after water, or else sit idly in camp. It was quickly decided to load the Thornycroft with the necessary food, water and petrol, and set out to a position on the map named Mount Marjory. From that position Lasseter would quickly tell whether his recorded bearings were correct. If his and Harding's watches had been correct on that day when they took bearings many years ago, all would be well. If not, then the party must return to Ilbilba and set out guided only by Lasseter's bushmanship and sense of locality.

The truck party's arrival synchronized with the coming of a handful of "desert rats". These wiry little savages rushed the soak with a shrieking chatter that drove the finches whirring to the trees. In an instant they were round the rock-hole, hand-lapping the water. The gobbling of the water sounded like tinkling tambourines. One desert boy in particular drank with particular gusto. He was going to be the giant of his tribe; a big, well-proportioned brat, he blew bubbles as gaspingly he drank his fill. Perhaps thinking he was blowing away too much moisture in bubbles, he grasped the rock-edge with both hands and, bending down, thrust his head into the water. His belly filled and swelled till it was like the udder of a cow. Still drinking, he uneasily spread his legs to give that distending stomach more room.

"Stand back," drawled Sutherland gravely, "he might back fire! If he springs a leak we'll get wet!"

This laughing, big-eyed kid they called "Bubbles". He soon laughed his way into the party's favour. They found he could eat as capably as he could laugh and drink.

These natives fill up like a camel with water when going to or coming from a desert trek. They can travel four days without water – the bucks considerably longer if necessary.

Taylor, in his insatiable thirst for curios, came to be the favourite of the natives. The party thought it was because he went amongst them clad only in boots, shorts and a hat. He became so brown that he looked like a native.

Naked piccaninnies spied the camp from cover – big-eyed kids who had never known a wash in their lives, their hair tangled with grass seeds and daubed in the ashes of campfires, their bellies protruding to a tremendous size.

The party, while treating the natives well, gave them no liberties. Some of these stone age men had seen their first whites only a few months before: others never before. The party wished to be on friendly terms with all the desert tribes. Their help might well be invaluable, while their hostility would mean unending anxiety if not disaster. The natives, however, were never allowed right within the camp; they were always quietly watched, and rarely given anything, unless they were asked to do some work. The party had no intention of turning itself into a philanthropic depot for wild myalls, and besides, familiarity breeds contempt. A contemptuous native is dangerous. Any food or small present given to them was always given from the truck, never from the supply dump. And care was taken that they did not learn the contents of the mysterious looking cases, bags, packages and tins that they looked at with awe. Thus it was hoped to work on their superstition when the party had to leave the supply dump unattended. The wild native will not touch what he does not understand: it is "Kaditcha".

One evening there was excitement amongst the natives. Micky took one glance across the plain and exclaimed: "By gum! Plenty feller camel he come!"

Wending snake-like among the spinifex were the grey forms of the old beasts of burden. They proved to be fifteen camels of Bob Buck's team, in charge of a native stockman who could read, write and speak almost perfect English. He had been brought up as a piccaninny in a South Australian home. Buck, the owner of Tempe Downs station, was the bushman who had packed the stores and cleared the 'drome for the Mackay expedition. When these map-makers left they discarded a number of petrol containers. The presence of the gold expedition at Ilbilba was a grand opportunity for Buck to send his natives the long distance to collect them.

Lasseter was delighted. The native stockman could speak a little of this particular desert "lingo" and with the head boy as interpreter the way was open for Lasseter to learn the language and much else besides. He used every opportunity.

The natives have no idea of counting. Any number above four they describe as "big feller mob". The party were to see how they solved the problem when compelled. Buck's hobbled camels fed over the plain by night, seeking desert grass among the spinifex and eating all but the porcupine spinifex itself. Among these camels there were the usual rogues that would wander for miles. Every morning a native stockman was sent out to round the mob up, otherwise some would surely stray to the wild camel herds. On returning to camp the man had to account for every camel. Squatting before the stockman in charge, he would pull out a number of pebbles and lay them solemnly one by one upon the ground to the following accompaniment: "This one feller Bluey. This one feller Micky. This one feller Judy. No, that one feller Rosy: this one feller Judy. This one feller Billy. This one feller Gutsacher (a notoriously greedy camel). This one feller Rowdy. No, that one Soldier: this one Rowdy. This one feller Toby. This one feller Kitty." And so on, until fifteen representative pebbles were laid at the boss stockman's feet.

7. THE FIRST TREK WEST

The party started west on a day so bright that the blueness of the sky almost hurt the eyes. Soon they were in the sandhills country, parallel ridges of sand rolling one after another like gigantic waves of an ocean. The truck slowly forged ahead, seeking channels between the ridges. Up these it crept, the sand so heavy that of ten they did not average three miles an hour; in ten days barely one hundred miles were covered.

Those countless ridges of vast age had almost hardened into sandstone. By no means all were pure sand; many were grey with stunted vegetation; an occasional striking patch of wild flowers looked like a bouquet upon a grey dress. A stillness all its own brooded over this country.

"You'd think the land was awaiting something," remarked Taylor. Lasseter's eyes shone.

The men often remarked on that stillness. And they were never tired of watching the sunrise spread like a breath of beauty over all the land. Australians have read of the desert sunsets of Egypt. But there are dawning and setting splendours on our own desert fringe that rival .those visions of beauty.

Lumbering down a precipitous "slideway", the Thornycroft broke two main leaves in the back spring, giving Taylor a job to anneal the broken springs and cut and convert them into spare leaves for the front springs. Presently, the heavy going broke them too. The party helped anxiously with each repair job. A severe mechanical breakdown might have disastrous consequences. The only water was what they carried.

"Motor-car he drink all a same two feller camel," Micky said, seriously.

"Well, if we are compelled to walk back, you have the best chance of reaching water," declared Blakeley.

"Myall black he spear me," answered Micky simply.

It was evident he had calculated all the chances. One day he pointed out a wisp of smoke rising lazily into the blue. Quickly it was answered by another many miles away, and then upon a further peak rose a gossamer thread.

"The stone age men are watching," said Blakeley.

"The beggars must be all around us," said Taylor. "And yet the country appears absolutely abandoned except for that smoke."

Micky was uneasy and unusually silent. He kept his eyes well open and slept as close to the whites as they would permit. He was not in joking humour, but the evening they camped more than usually late he provided a laugh. Sutherland was dishing out the tucker. He had to rake the things out by firelight. Micky was prompt for his share, and Sutherland handed him a hunk of damper with meat; then, remembering there was still a lump of cheese somewhere about, he rooted round in the tucker-box for it. The men were hungrily at work when Taylor said:

"What on earth's happened to Micky. He's foaming at the mouth!" Micky *was* foaming; his face was screwed up in speechless disgust.

"What's wrong, Micky?" inquired Sutherland; "don't you like the cheese?"

"Tchese be dam," spat Micky. "This plurry soap!"

It was with keen anticipation that they arrived within seven miles of sombre Mount Marjory. From there Lasseter might well look on his promised land. Miles of rock-filled gullies barred the Thornycroft's further progress. Early next morning Blakeley and Lasseter set out to scale the mountain. They arrived at its northern base and climbed two thousand feet, to stare up a wall rising sheer eight hundred feet to a great cap of rock that sat flat upon the summit. They found a wallaby-pad which trailed like a thread up the lip of the crevice. On hands and knees they crawled to within two hundred feet of the top and found the face of the cliff scarred deep as if riven by the storms of ages. Massive boulders rested shakily here; rock ledges were rotten and powdery.

It took them two hours to crawl back down the wallaby-pad. They then crept around the mountain cap and found that the western side sloped up. Breathing thankful relief at the easier climbing, they gained the flat summit and looked out over the world, feeling very small. Through an ocean of blue they gazed far away down where, miles distant, there dazzled the salt-encrusted bottom of Lake McDonald, spreading for shimmering miles into faint salt swamps. Eighty miles south was a serrated area of sand-ridges that took their breath away. Surely nothing but an aeroplane could cross those ridges! Above them a magic picture floated in the sky. A mirage had thrown, as on a screen, the Petermann Ranges, at least 150 miles away. Lasseter gazed and gazed, seeking some familiar landmark, some mountain, something. Then he spread out his instruments and pored over them, carefully making his calculations.

"We are 150 miles too far north," he said at last. "The watches were wrong!"

Blakeley stood gazing far across that uninhabited vastness of Centralia. The oldest country in the world had been calmly waiting since the beginning of Time. Time! Time meant nothing to it. And yet a mistake in two tiny watches thirty years ago meant so much to these modern lords of creation, so desperately dependent on Time. They climbed down the southern side, an awful enough experience that landed them on a plain covered with rocks and dry, creviced watercourses.

At the foot of a sombre bluff that rose three thousand feet were two desert men's graves. Twenty tons of stone were built into a tomb, terraced around with stones. The sleepers' feet faced the east, for closely packed pebbles on the bosom of the tomb outlined the bodies. Each warrior's arms lay by his right hand, stone knives, stone spear heads, stone hammers. They must have been chiefs of tribes who thus lay in state. The white men gazed up at the black cliffs whose shadow was already over the grave, wondering if the warriors had slipped and met their death while chasing game on those dizzy ledges above, or whether with those stone knives they had fought a duel up there for some dusky belle of the desert, while the tribe clustered breathless below. After a ten-mile walk to beat the setting sun, the men rejoined the Thornycroft, to find their mates very anxious.

The men's faces were intent and thoughtful as they quietly discussed the position. Blakeley believed that the car could not penetrate farther; their observations had practically proved that. The best plan was to return to Ilbilba and from there set out in a new direction, trusting to Lasseter's bushmanship to guide them to their goal.

"Go on!" urged Lasseter. "Carry on. Never turn back. Time, petrol, food, water, mean everything. Strike a new course from here."

"Seems to me," drawled Sutherland, "we've come to the midways track. Carry on if we can. If not, return to Ilbilba and set out from there, as originally intended."

This counsel was agreed upon. Taylor was cheerfully prepared to carry on or turn back and carry on again, just as his comrades decided. In the following days they penetrated another twenty miles farther; but an ocean of deep sand-ridges, apparently without end, finally blocked all movement of the truck. Beaten, they set back on the long return to Ilbilba.

Arrived at Ilbilba, they found Colson was ten days overdue. Anxiously they debated the possibility of his having met with an accident. Perhaps he was lying helpless, fighting the ants anywhere along that lonely three-hundred-mile stretch to Alice Springs. And the party could not move on their new venture without a further supply of petrol and stores.

They were surprised .to see five camels feeding on the plain, while at a new camp near the depot a white man was bending over a fire. He strolled cheerfully towards them. A young chap, well built, with a springy step, he looked tough. He introduced himself as Paul Johns, a dingo shooter. Had heard of the big gold expedition while at Hermannsburg, and just drifted along. Hoped they didn't mind. The party were not sure. However, they didn't own the country, and if this nomad was there – well, he was there, that was all. Future events would decide their attitude. They had heard of Johns at Alice Springs. A runaway sailor from a German ship, he had proved a wanderer on land. Three years previously he had drifted to Alice Springs. In that district he had secured five camels, and the services of two natives, and set out as a dingo shooter and poisoner. He had roamed some wild country. In payment for stray articles wandering natives sometimes put him on to ranges where wild dogs were thickest. He laid his baits, and the natives tracked the stricken dogs and speared those with life still in them. Thus he rarely missed a dog. Getting, of necessity, most of his game around rock-holes and native wells he was rapidly learning his way about both ranges and desert. At long intervals he disposed of his scalps at Alice Springs, buying stores and ammunition. He looked the makings of a bushman, this sun-browned smiler.

His two "boys" were exceptional travellers, so far as an aboriginal's travel is concerned. They had come in close contact with different tribes and knew quite a smattering of languages. This pleased Lasseter. The party also took advantage of it when natives, curious to see their first white man, came into camp. Blakeley closely questioned old Rip Van Winkle, now, as to soaks along their proposed south-west route.

Rip Van had brought his two wives and numerous offspring into camp. (Strangely enough, in the light of after events, two of the children were cripples.) He exhibited this brood of the desert with pride. It was plain Rip considered them *the* family of those parts. As time wore on they were to understand better Rip Van, his family, and his tribe. He and one other man with his family were all that remained of a desert tribe; the others had been exterminated by desert warfare and some strange disease. Rip Van had his life's work cut out. He was filled with burning zeal to rear his tribe up again. The oldest lesson of Nature and the strongest urge of man were exemplified in this skinny-shanked desert man, terrified lest the age-old traditions of his tribe die with him and be utterly forgotten. And he had only two wives to build up with; to steal other women would mean bringing added wrath upon his head. Whether he proved capable of laying a successful foundation for the gradual rebuilding of his people is an interesting question.

With the aid of Johns's natives, "sand maps" were drawn, Rip Van being eloquent with his thick, horny finger-nail in making depressions along the proposed route where soakages would be found. The party proved later on that where that old rascal indicated a soak forty miles north, that soak was forty miles south. All the semi-desert and desert tribes were the same. Understandably so. Their very lives depend on their cunningly concealed rock waterholes. At long distances apart across that region are circular wells in solid rock, or soaks in dry creeks. Any hunting party, after a three days march without water, coming to one of these wells and finding it dry, would be almost certainly doomed. Those strongest ones who could still travel day and night to the next waterhole would live; that was all. The aborigines never dig more soaks or improve existing ones. They are content with the immemorial reservoirs found by their forefathers.

Fred Blakely questions Rip Van Winkle.

8. THE FLIGHT OF THE *GOLDEN QUEST*

Uncertainty drove the party to action, for Colson did not arrive. Lasseter, with Micky, stayed by the stores at Ilbilba. Blakeley, Sutherland and Taylor got aboard the Thornycroft and set off once again back along their tracks. The natives followed them for miles, bent almost double, excitedly pointing, in wide-eyed amazement at the making track.

This track was a source of unending interest to them, far more so than the truck itself. That is understandable. From the time these children of the desert are born, their eyes look down for tracks – tracks of things to eat, of everything that walks or crawls or touches the ground before it flies. Friend or foe, by tracks do the desert children know them. Tracks are their book of life.

Rip Van Winkle, pointing to the broad track of the tyres, had told the party of how a nomad and his wives, cutting across the desert into the fringe, had stared aghast at this monstrous track of the unknown. The family had hurried back along the track forty miles, afraid to cross it.

The native sees far more in a track than we do. He can name the person who made it, provided he has seen the maker's tracks before. He can tell many other material facts besides. After which, his inborn superstition comes in. He imbues the track with a "personality". That is the best word to describe it. The track of a man, or of anything, retains an essence of personality even though many days old. And that essence in the track can possibly harm, and the maker of the track can be harmed. The witch-doctors will dig up the clay of a man's track and "charm" it through the "personality" still adhering to it. Similarly with a man's finger-nails, or the clippings of hair from his head or beard. Carefully they burn those clippings lest the "personality" in it be "charmed" against the owner.

Absurd, of course. Still, in some points, perhaps, faintly correct. We know that a dog by smell can follow a track, even one day old. The smell of the person lingers though the track may have vanished. So animals trace their strayed young. Then there is that queer practice of the whites, psychometry, by which mediumistic people claim they can, by handling any object, tell events that occurred to the owner of it. Some vaguely realized sense acting on the "personality" left by the owner reveals these things to the medium.

The three men wondered whether they would find Colson at Taylor's

Creek. They felt that a hoodoo hung over the place. When they reached the creek he was not there. Many miles farther back they met him, overjoyed that he was safe. Unavoidable delays had kept him at Alice Springs.

Colson brought great news. The directors had sent another 'plane. Pilot Pat Hall was flying it. He would arrive at Ilbilba as soon as possible with Coote, who had recovered from his injuries, except for a limp. This was cheery news. In the best of spirits the men unloaded the stores from the auxiliary truck on to the Thornycroft. Colson's orders were to return direct to Alice Springs, load up with the remainder of the supplies, and at once return to Ilbilba with definite news as to the date of Hall's arrival in the *Golden Quest II.*

Travelling was easy along their old tracks. The Thornycroft was driven practically day and night lest the 'plane should arrive before them at Ilbilba. But it did not.

Lasseter received the news of the anticipated second 'plane very happily. With its assistance he would fly in hours over country it would take the truck weeks to cover. He would fly right to his country, locate landmarks, and spy out a track for the truck; so saving time, money and supplies. Nine days of waiting followed, the party growing more anxious as day after cloudless day went by.

While Lasseter was busy at every opportunity learning the natives' speech, they were picking up scraps of English – especially stray swear words. Those are always the first the natives acquire. Some among them, in perfect mimicry, could repeat instantly the words the white man had just used. Once, when Sutherland was trying to explain to a big-nosed native that a fork was to be used for eating purposes and not to pick his toe-nails with, he added exasperatedly, "You stupid-looking parrot, why don't you — well Jerry!"

"You stupid-looking parrot, why don't you — well Jerry!" repeated the man instantly, and his tribesmen roared appreciation.

"That plurry nigger swear too plurry much," observed Micky, reprovingly. "Him too plurry cheeky altogether."

He of the fork and toe-nails must have partly understood what Sutherland had been driving at, for, scorning to look at Micky, he asked Sutherland for "a hand out". But that spare gentleman drew himself to his full height, pulled up his shirt, and, holding his breath, laid his hands pathetically upon his hollowed stomach. Those ribs told their own tale. The tribesmen grunted sympathy. They could understand hunger and its effects.

That sundown a group of them stood some distance from the camp, evidently arguing amongst themselves as to the white man's words.

"Those nigs," remarked Taylor to Sutherland, "are calling us all the —'s they can think of."

"Those nigs," shouted back a voice in surprising mimicry, "callem us all a —'s him can think of." And a howl of laughter greeted the surprise of the white men.

Micky scowled at this further exhibition of "cheek", but like the good dog who knows his bones, he did not go outside and bark at the dingoes.

Yet another desert-stained band of nomads, hearing of the mysterious white men, and anxious to see what made the wonderful tracks across the sandhills, came into Ilbilba. Their sophisticated brethren clothed them in a wisp of rag and a circlet of tobacco-tin lids. Bubbles, sure of his welcome, introduced them to the camp. Sutherland gave Bubbles a bellyfull of stew, a hunk of damper, and a tin of boiling tea. Then, taking the pipe from his mouth, he spat gravely and handed the child a looking-glass. Bubbles turned into a serious-visaged piccaninny immediately he caught his own laughing face in the glass. He stared as if at the devil; his eyes bulged like black marbles; his mouth opened to yell, but just wouldn't. His compatriots waited in a strained silence, apprehensive at the effect on the child. Sutherland smoked and scratched his ear. The child woke up. Drawing a deep breath, he dropped the damper, and, staring into the mirror, stealthily crept his hand to the back. His lips shut tight as he grabbed.

Those clutching fingers closed on air, and he stared into the glass as if petrified. An ominous murmur broke from the tribesmen. What fresh devilry was this? Had these white devils bewitched the piccaninny? Suddenly the child ducked his head around behind the glass. Taylor bit his lip at the amazement of the kid. Trembling a little, the child stared into the glass again, then very craftily edged his face past the mirror until one big brown eye peeped behind, staring amazed into space. Taylor burst out laughing. The tribesmen sprang erect, angrily grunting. As they strode muttering away the child dropped the glass and sped after them with his damper.

Just before dark they heard the hum of Colson's truck, and, springing from the shed, saw his headlights coming like giant fireflies far across the plain.

"The *Golden Quest II* is due to-morrow," said Colson, as they put the billy on. Sure enough, in the following afternoon they heard the drone of the 'plane. The smoke signals were lit and the natives came around, staring up impassively at the giant bird of which they had heard so much. But as that "bird" swooped down nearly every man ran for cover. The 'plane landed perfectly and the whites eagerly welcomed her.

The black men crawled from their cubby-holes to first examine the tracks the 'plane made on landing. Curiously enough, they found far more of interest in the truck than the 'plane. The truck made tracks; they could trail it across the ground. But who could follow the flight of a bird!

Pat Hall was a slim young Aussie, a well-known Victorian pilot. His air of lively curiosity and fresh news of the far-away world acted like a tonic on the party; that was why, perhaps, at the evening meal Sutherland solicitously tendered him the choicest piece of meat. Hall, merrily chatting, hacked off a lump rather doubtfully.

"Take it in your hand and chew," advised Sutherland, "like the niggers do. We dine *a la mode* here."

Hall complied, attempted a bite, and held on with his teeth while dragging the lump away with his fists. White sinews gleamed from the meat which slipped and catapulted back on his nose.

"Desert wallaby is tough," munched Sutherland. "Try again."

But Hall laughed. He wasn't very hungry, he explained. Next morning Hall took Lasseter on a flight to spy out the country. It was the happiest ride of Lasseter's life. As the 'plane droned on he gazed down upon his promised land. They sped across broad vistas of sandhill and mulga and spinifex, then over mountain tops whose serrated faces looked up from canyons and valleys and rugged chasms that took Hall's breath away. Fancy a forced landing on those rugged escarpments and miles of broken pinnacles! Lasseter stared down, smiling to himself, the cool air kissing his face. Then the country ridged out into sandhills again, with spreading patches of sand. The 'plane dived low, giving Lasseter every chance to study the country. They 'planed over isolated oases of green timber, in each of which were plainly seen the white ashes of native fires. They skimmed over two mountains rising liked rocky horns from the earth, then dived down again to see country very interesting to the prospector or geologist – white outcrops of quartz upon ridges of apparently red iron sand. Whether that is a strip of mineralized country covered during the course of ages by drifting sand, Time and prospecting only will tell.

They skirted the edge of a dry lake stretching far away amid stunted black vegetation, and hummed over vistas of sand and ridges until Lasseter leaned excitedly forward. The sand-ridges had changed direction! It was one identification mark he wished imperatively to see. They 'planed down until at times the wheels were nearly skimming the ground. Two snow-white cockatoos gossiping on a tree-top left their perch hurriedly. Hall laughed. It seemed funny. He could plainly see the outraged crests of the birds as they dodged the machine. "Water must be handy," mused Lasseter. Those two were the only cockatoos they saw on the whole flight.

Eager for fresh conquests, Hall swooped low over a clump of trees from which he glimpsed a curl of smoke. The roar of the 'plane drowned terrified shrieks as a mob of naked blacks leapt up and scattered in all directions. Laughing heartily at how he had spoiled their dinner, Hall laughed more at a piccaninny who fell sprawling and, too frightened to rise, lay kicking on the sand.

Presently Lasseter turned round and passed Hall a note saying he had identified landmarks. They came around and flew back to camp, covering country in a few hours which would have taken a truck many weary days to traverse.

That was one successful trip done by the 'planes during the expedition. Eagerly his mates gathered around Lasseter as he stepped from the 'plane and told them he had located the outskirts of the country. Fresh hopes of a quick and successful completion to their task brought smiles again to their faces and a jauntiness of step which the stone age watchers quickly commented upon. But disappointment followed almost instantly. The two airmen, after consultation, decided that the cruising range of the *Golden Quest II* (three hundred and eighty miles) was dangerously short over such a vast country, with no chance of help for many days if there should be a forced landing. They decided that in the interests and safety of the party the 'plane should be flown to Adelaide, her Cirrus Mark II engine changed to a Gypsy Mark I, and a larger petrol tank installed to give a range of seven hundred and fifty miles. The airmen would fly the 'plane to Adelaide via Alice Springs. Pilot Coote would return as soon as possible with the reconditioned 'plane.

The men, faced with another long wait in a camp now harassed by myriads of flies, did not say much. What was the use? They joked, though, when next morning the footprints of a native were found corning right up to the bunk of a sleeper. They examined the track apprehensively; the farthest footprint showed where the savage had actually bent towards the bunk, then, hesitating, turned away. Visions of a spear stab while he slept flashed across the mind of each man there. One of Johns's boys was quietly called up and put on to the tracks. The blackfellow bent over them, then looked up with a broadening smile.

"Him track belonga lubra!" he said slyly.

Relieved laughter broke the tension. The honour of the lady's visit was promptly accorded to the airmen both of whom had been noticed to step sideways when a native woman passed by, "because they smell so!"

However, it was decided that a sharper watch than usual should be kept at night. The knowledge that a native could come right within the camp unheard and unseen was accepted as a warning.

Hall and Coote flew off. The men, standing in a little group, watched them go, Lasseter with a grimness that was almost a sneer.

"Fly away, birdie, fly away," drawled Sutherland.

Lasseter turned abruptly and walked off. Blakeley was worried. Inaction in this place would certainly get on the nerves of all concerned. Besides, it meant additional expense for the company. His eyes fell on Colson and he made up his mind to send the auxiliary back to Alice Springs with word to the directors that the Thornycroft would push on towards the limit of the country scouted by the 'plane. Colson would return to Ilbilba, pick up water and petrol, and follow the track of the truck. Thus the party would be well ahead with the task, perhaps even into the country Lasseter had recognized, before Coote returned from Adelaide.

The others eagerly acceded to the plan. Paul Johns, too, was "pushing out." He said farewell with a friendly smile. The others watched him go rather dubiously. They were not sure how far he was going. If he intended to track them up –

9. MYSTERY AND MAGIC

Perhaps this chapter does not directly concern the result of the expedition; perhaps it does. Maybe it could remain unwritten without affecting the story. However, I will write it, because the subject greatly interested the men concerned (they discuss it even more now) and because it may prove interesting to readers – especially those with a taste for uncanny things and anthropology. What is recorded here actually happened.

The morning after Johns left Ilbilba, the party became aware that something was amiss over at the native camp. All there were in a high state of nervous excitement. Rip Van in particular was prowling round the camp and up to the soak and back, hands clenched behind his back, head bent towards the ground, muttering and swaying his body from side to side. The natives were obviously panic-stricken; they quite ignored the whites and their questions. Throughout the day, a crouching group on a hill above the spring were earnestly reading smoke signals. That night they vanished.

Next morning a desert tribe, total strangers, arrived. Lasseter; with Micky, happened to be away from camp, prospecting. The tribe halted and consulted; then half a dozen men came diffidently towards the white men's camp. They halted a hundred yards distant while the leader walked forward making signs of peace, of water, of food and of "sit down". Then he spread his arms towards his tribesmen and they all knelt and buried their weapons in the sand. A little band of naked men then walked slowly towards the whites.

They were welcomed; they had to be. Here was a fresh tribe of arrant myalls, and here was the party on the point of vacating the camp and leaving the supplies. The leader was given water in a fruit tin. They stared at the tin, volubly admiring its beauty. Then they attempted to drink. The leader dipped his fingers into the tin to lap the water up with his mouth. Sutherland showed them how to drink: It was funny to see them trying to manipulate the jagged edge. They howled laughing when a comrade cut his tongue. They could not balance the vessel, and thought it the greatest joke in the world when one spilled the water down his chest. Having got them in a good humour, a slice of bread and meat was dished out to each man. But shaggy brows frowned suspiciously. Lasseter, just then returned, had to take a bite of each man's bread and meat before they could eat. When they did, they enjoyed it. Their eyes rolled; they shook their heads and talked volubly with their mouths full; it was plainly wonderful food.

They wanted more. The present of a few shattered pieces of glass cemented the friendship when it was shown them how the glass would scrape their spear points sharp.

The presence of these natives was responsible for the party taking an unwitting part in a tragic little desert drama. The incident may shed light on a perhaps ethnological fact of native life.

Three mornings later, these desert nomads began to act most peculiarly. They were sullen; would answer no questions; would not talk above a whisper. They could not keep their eyes off one direction. They had developed a frightened hostility. But for the life of him Blakeley could not be sure whether the hostility was against the whites or not. This was a serious position, as the party was almost ready to vacate camp. Blakeley went amongst the natives, but they would have nothing to do with him.

Blakeley told the party no man must leave camp. Every man must remain armed and quietly await events. Just then Micky, who had gone for water, hurried into camp with his eyes nearly starting from his head.

"Kaditcha!" he gasped. "Man in Kaditcha shoes he walk about! We go away quick feller!" Micky's veneer of civilization had vanished. He had slipped back into the stone age from which he had never really emerged.

"Oh, well," said Lasseter, "if it's a Kaditcha then it has nothing to do with us."

"But what is this particular Kaditcha?" asked Taylor. "What does he mean by the 'man in the Kaditcha shoes'?"

"They're shoes," explained Lasseter, "of emu feathers clotted together with blood. The shoes are so made that their imprint gives no indication whether the wearer is coming or going. Thus, a foe cannot track him, even if any native were game to attempt such tracking. Only men whom the stars have favoured are able to wear the shoes. Some stars, you know, are believed to be ancestors of the natives. The power necessary to wear the shoes is given the Kaditcha man by the spirits of the dead. While such a man is wearing them he is imbued with superhuman powers. Evidently an enemy of this tribe has walked around their camp in the night, encircling it with an invisible band of evil. It is the finding of these tracks that has made the natives so nervous. I'll bet they'll vacate the waterhole. That, most likely, is what the Kaditcha man wants. The effect of the Kaditcha tracks on them is the same as a ghost at a waterhole would be on us. We'd want to leave!"

All day the natives clung together; throughout the afternoon they kept whispering; at sundown a chant broke out, peculiarly low and soft. At twilight the men, in a compact body, suddenly appeared right at the white men's fire. From away out in the darkness came a haunting croon from the lubras and children. One fine athletic savage bent over Taylor, gesticulating and whispering, making imploring advances.

"He wants you to go with him," interpreted Lasseter. "He has something great and sacred the tribe wishes to present to us through you."

The party held a quick consultation. The natives were in deadly earnest. They listened with a terrible eagerness, with almost a fear of death on their faces. Whatever their object, should they be frustrated it might inevitably bring on the conflict the party wished so ardently to avoid.

"You go with him, Phil," decided Blakeley. "You are armed and he is not. Shoot him should he lead you into danger."

Taylor and the native departed, to the relieved delight of the tribesmen. A great weight seemed to have been taken from their shoulders. They squatted close around the fire, shoulder to shoulder, whispering occasionally, waiting. The croon of the hidden women never ceased; it sounded almost a prayer.

There was not a sound from the night, save that ghostly croon. Had Taylor been treacherously murdered? The party dared not go and see. Perhaps the natives had actually planned to split them up. They might be prepared to spring upon them now, while others crept up behind. Fully armed, the men waited and listened. Mick was in a blue funk.

An hour passed. Then the tribesmen with one accord turned their heads, peering with excited whisperings. Soon Taylor's footsteps were heard. With the native guide he strode excitedly to the fire.

The native was carrying something bulky and long. As the firelight gleamed upon it the tribesmen bowed their heads to the ground. The native squatted by the fire, balancing upon his palms a flat hardwood stick some twelve feet in length, six inches wide and half an inch thick. Its edges tapered like a two-edged sword. The stick was remarkably carved from end to end.

"A wonderful curio," said Taylor eagerly, as the party examined it. "I've never seen anything like it, and I've been round the world and in queer places."

The carvings resembled the vivid markings of a diamond snake. But as the men looked closer they saw that the carvings, in their recurring squares and series of rings, were all of varying patterns, sizes, and depths of colour. A breath from all the ages seemed to come from that dull flat stick. It seemed older by far than the pyramids; the hands of countless people had fondled it; eyes when humanity was young had jealously watched it; reverent voices of long dead thousands had crooned over it.

Its presence seemed to bring the breath of the tomb, and yet it looked indestructible.

The natives, not one of whom had dared to stand up, shuffled like crabs into a squatting semicircle close around the tribesman holding the stick. An old, old man squatted opposite the stick, his grey head bowed, his trembling arms raised over the emblem. His body began swaying from side to side as he crooned the opening notes of a low chant. The tribesmen joined in with the lead, stretching out their arms, with bowed heads and swaying bodies, their voices pausing to join again with the old man's croon. Only the young warrior with the stick held his head erect and stared at the whites as he crooned. His muscular body, with the cicatrices of warriorhood across his chest, his piercing eyes, exemplified youth and life in contrast with the bowed old greybeard before him.

The whites looked on in silent amazement while the performers wedged themselves almost completely around the stick, the arms of those behind supplicating over the bowed forms in front. Two rows of hands then gently swayed backwards and forwards a little above the stick.

It was a most solemn affair, rather wonderful in the firelight. Then the old man, still softly crooning, tried hard for many minutes to convey something to the whites. The others, ceaselessly crooning, helped his plaint with imploring, expressive eyes.

"They want us to do exactly as they do," interpreted Lasseter. He then squatted on the right side of the old man and spread his arms over the stick. Delight sang in the chant as Taylor immediately squatted on the left of the old man, while, to the encouraging nod of the natives, Blakeley and Sutherland did likewise. Micky crouched away in abject fear.

The old master of ceremonies glared strangely at Lasseter. The tribesmen's chant changed to a weird dirge, each word slow and distinct, heads nodding in time to the pronunciation. Lasseter eagerly joined in. Here was a golden opportunity of learning not only strange new words but an obviously sacred custom as well. Taylor joined in hesitatingly; then Blakeley and Sutherland as they got the monotonous croon of the thing. It was a remarkable scene, those crouching, swaying blacks and whites in the glow of the camp-fire under the desert stars. The strangest part of it all is its truth.

As the white men gradually got the time and pronunciation, the black faces opposite expressed joy unbounded as they looked to the stars and nodded to the stick. So vividly was that chant impressed on the memory that Blakeley had it written down before dawn. Finally, the old man signed to Lasseter to spread his hands on the broad stick. Lasseter did so; then Taylor; then the others, distinctly conscious of an eerie, expectant note in the chant.

Slowly, the warrior holding the stick began to withdraw his palms, as he did so signing Lasseter to place his palms underneath, finger-tip to finger-tip with the warrior. As his palms glided away so Lasseter's slid forward while his mate's finger-tips gripped the stick edges. As the warrior slid his hands away the stick was left resting on the palms of Lasseter. Instantly the chant ceased, and in the strained silence there went up a sigh of intense relief. As one man, the natives stealthily crept back, still facing the stick. On their finger-tips and toes they backed away into the night, like giant baboons. Then the croon of the lubras ceased.

Only the man who had held the stick remained. He stood erect now, with the light of a great triumph in his eyes, and walked away, signing to Taylor to bring the stick. Completely mystified, Taylor did so. When out of sight of the firelight the warrior feverishly scraped a long hole in the sand. He covered it in peculiar fashion with spinifex grass; then, stepping aside so that the stick could not touch him, he signed to Taylor to lay the sacred stick in the hole. Taylor did so. The warrior took a handful of sand, and, waving it over the stick, let the sand shower softly down. He whispered as he crouched over the stick, and the falling of the sand was like the sighing of wind through the desert oak by night. Again and again he showered the stick until it was completely covered. Then, upon the outline of the sand, he placed leaves and grass stalks all patterned like the markings of a snake. Springing erect, with his shoulders braced as if he were reborn, he strode abruptly into the darkness without a backward glance. Taylor waited a while, then dug up the stick and hurried with it to camp.

"What on earth does it all mean?" they each asked.

"It is not a churinga," mused Blakeley. "Their sacred churingas are sticks and stones seldom more than eight inches long. This has some far greater significance than that."

"It's the greatest curio I've ever seen," said Taylor, admiringly. "Don't let on about it. Some day this big beauty is going to hang above the mantelpiece of a little home in Yorkshire. Here, Micky – why, what on earth!"

Micky was crouched almost out in the shadows, in terror.

"Sposem women see that one, he die!" he mumbled. "Maybe we die, too!" And he crept away to his blanket.

They did not laugh, knowing quite well that for a woman to see some of the sacred ceremonies and churingas of any tribe means death to her who should not look.

"It is a great prize," said Lasseter; "I wish I knew what it all means."

He and Taylor sewed canvas securely around the stick, padding it against chance of disfigurement. Its width and length made it very awkward.

"I'll make a special fastener for it on the side of the truck," said Taylor. "I'm going to get this thing away to civilization and back home."

Next morning there was not a sign of a native.

"I'll bet they have travelled all through the night," said Blakeley, "which is what the Australian aboriginal seldom does."

10. THE DEAD-END

One glorious morning the party set off on their new course south-west. The Thornycroft was humming along with an occasional bump over tufted spinifex and ant hills; all was going splendidly; everything in order. Taylor dodged a mulga tree, then, rumbling out into a patch of open country, the crew roared:

> Sailing up the Clyde, sailing up the Clyde,
> Home to Bonnie Scotland where the old folks bide.

Two didn't join in the singing. Blakeley was worried, and stared thoughtfully ahead. The party was a long way behind schedule; and the crash of the *Golden Quest I* had been a bad setback and expense. The reconditioning of the second 'plane meant further lost time and much additional expense. The help that all had counted on from the 'plane as a scout was not available. The error in Lasseter's bearings, too, although partly anticipated, had caused a long and arduous trip in vain. In this present trip, they knew by Hall's flight that desert lay ahead over which it was doubtful that the truck could pass.

Lasseter, too, sat staring grimly ahead. He knew the difficulties the ground-party was up against. From the 'plane he had recognized not quite his country – the 'plane could not cruise that far – but mountain landmarks on the edge of it.

The party instinctively knew his thoughts. He was going on. Each setback had made the man grimmer, more savagely determined. Without speaking of it they realized that, no matter what happened, this man would not be beaten.

Taylor, at his beloved wheel, thought how wonderfully the sun brightened the valleys, turned the sand-ridges to gold, and made even the drab vegetation look gay. He dodged concealed crevices, picked out the hardest patches of sand, instinctively appearing to know just where to expect broken ground, while keeping the big truck at an easy maximum speed over the rapidly altering contours of country. Now and then he broke into light-hearted song. He was the first white man ever to sing there. Sutherland pulled at his smelly old pipe, his sarcastic, but never hurtful, wit occasionally applauding Taylor's efforts, cheeking Blakeley, or having a sly dig at Lasseter. Always the tact and never-failing good humour of the man kept the party together and did much to lighten disappointments.

"You no fall off now, Micky," he laughed. "You stick alla same tree longa hill."

Micky grinned.

"See that sthone over there," and Sutherland pointed to a distant mountain. "Sposem you have motor truck, sposem camel too; which one you take along that sthone?"

"Camel more better," answered Micky soberly. "Motor-car 'puff-puff' alla same a plurry goanna, fallem back over plurry head all time same a plurry ants!"

The passing days brought them into sterner desert country. Its vegetation, its beauty even, surprised the men. The pitted sand betrayed the passing of a shower of rain; the tufted spinifex and occasional shrubbery were clothed in sombre green. Occasionally in the flat distances they would see a beautiful desert-gum or oak rearing high its lordly self, an attraction to the eye for miles. They were boyishly delighted at the grasses and blaze of wildflowers.

"Flower out here in the dinkum desert," exclaimed Taylor enthusiastically. "Why, we might even see game! Hasn't anyone noticed tracks?"

"They are looking at you," drawled Sutherland, "right beside your own big feet."

Taylor stared down; "Rats!" he said.

"No, ants," replied Sutherland, and with a straw he pointed out tiny tracks of feet – the parasite ant.

These ants grow their own meat. They bite the legs off members of their species and turn them into living silos. Then they concentrate their energies on feeding their voracious victims. These grow extraordinarily fat like blubbery lumps of meat, and in winter time the ants eat them.

The truck ploughed on. Its labouring became a roar in that land of waiting silences. Occasionally the sandhills were of almost hard red brick sandstone; evidence of vast age. Trees had grown upon them, for stumps like petrified teeth protruded from the steep brown sides. By the Western Australian border, limestone hillocks and pans sprang up, and weird ironstone conglomerates like plastered hillocks in a giants' playground.

"Something has got on Micky's goat," said Sutherland.

"The stick!" volunteered Lasseter.

"He's a changed man," said Taylor. "Do you notice he won't go near the side of the truck where the stick is strapped on? He won't even walk around that side of the truck."

"He would have deserted at Ilbilba had he dared," said Blakeley, "only he knew the other natives would have speared him. We won't hold him a moment when he gets a chance to go in safety."

On a night of silver shadows the party were sprawled around the camp-fire, Sutherland humming a song about "a shanty by the creek". Taylor and Blakeley were light-heartedly chiacking Micky. Their gay spirits were a cloak. Each man realized that the sands were hemming them in. Lasseter stood up and walked abruptly out into the night. Such a glorious night! All around and above was the faintest blue through which a man could see a surprising distance. The sandhills were silver-gold. The night felt friendly to Lasseter; almost it seemed awaiting him; it wrapped him round and he walked on into it, his footfalls faintly musical. He walked quite a distance then stood staring out over the land. Its rolling hillocks and shadows were beautiful under the stars and a faint moon. His gaze was suddenly attracted towards a steep ridge to his right, upon which, in prick-eared silhouette, there walked a dingo. Lasseter stared at the first animal seen on this trip. The wild dog stopped on the very crest of the ridge, sat on his haunches, slowly lifted his head, and howled at the moon. That mournful howl froze the very marrow in Lasseter's bones. Again the dingo howled. The long-drawn hopelessness in that sound seemed to come from the very belly of despair. Lasseter cursed the dog and returned along his tracks. He could not dismiss an awful feeling that identified himself with that yearning howl.

They came to the "Breakaway Country", a land of hard sandstone formation, shattered in broken layers like the bed of a dried-up sea. A little later they all stood upon a hill and gazed into the end of their journey.

Over a brink that stretched away to right and left like the lip of the world was a drop of 300 feet down on to sandy wastes. Three miles farther the sand rose abruptly up into more desolate wastes. Miles farther rose another ledge, and then sand, sand, sand. The riven earth appeared to have been thrust up and then fallen in cliff – like plains of stone intersected by sandy wastes.

Lasseter was standing staring out from the highest point of the bank.

"We'll call this 'Lasseter's Lookout'," whispered Sutherland.

The others nodded. Words were not needed; the country was impassable. They held a consultation.

"I doubt if untold labour, money, and block and tackle would do it," said Blakeley at last. "I doubt if even camels could find a way across. What say you, Phil?"

"I am the last man in the world to say turn back," answered Taylor, slowly. "But, speaking as an engineer, if you take the truck in there you will never get it back."

Sutherland agreed. Micky's silence was more eloquent than words.

"I am going on!" said Lasseter.

His comrades stared at him.

"How?" asked Blakeley at last.

"By camel!" said Lasseter.

Blakeley turned, gazing far away back towards Ilbilba. "I have it," he said in that slow way of his. "Johns! He has five camels and is hanging around Ilbilba somewhere. You take Johns, load the camels with supplies and water and push on if you wish. The rest of us will return to Alice Springs, where I will wire the directors. We will probably return to Sydney. That will cut down expenses at least sixty per cent, and allow you all the more time and capital to carry on. What say you?"

"That will do me!" said Lasseter with a smile.

"It's a strange thing," said Blakeley, slowly. "Utter barrenness lies before us and yet it might hold wealth untold. I'm not thinking of gold. Geologists say oil is squeezed by pressure from strata into porous storage beds, such as sandstone. Well, we see enough sandstone before us, heaven knows. They say, again, that earth movements produced the folding in which the oil accumulates. Well, look at those smashed up ledges running into the distance, plain evidence that the earth about here has been very busy in ages past. They say oil came from forests and vegetation. Well, there are petrified forests in Centralia, proving seas of vegetation in past ages. Oil men cite limestone in relation to oil. Well, we have passed over plenty of limestone. They say, too, the formation took place probably at the bottom of a sea. Well, there are enough huge dried-up salt-lakes all around us to prove that Centralia was once the bed of a sea."

"Sounds rather conclusive," said Taylor. "Let us bore for oil!"

"Let us bore for nuts," smiled Sutherland.

They had hardly returned to Ilbilba when Johns arrived. Arrangements were quickly made. He was very willing to accompany Lasseter. His camels were in good trim; he himself desired the trip. All was arranged.

The supply depot was made as safe as possible. During their absence, local natives had returned but had not touched a thing, though their tracks were thick around the dump. The party got busy loading the truck for the return to Alice Springs, and apportioning the supplies for the camel party. In the midst of the bustle their preparations were nearly brought to a premature end.

Down from the soak came a bunch of nomads, wild as their spinifex wastes. They were led forward by the irrepressible Bubbles, while the local tribesmen stood around the party, clearly expecting them to greet courteously the strangers. Among these was a young lubra, her tousled hair plaited with grass, her eyes bright with fear. She trod like a cat on hot bricks as she stepped fearfully forward. She was arrayed for the occasion, an opportunist warrior having "dressed" her with a figleaf from somebody's cast-off shirt.

This wild young thing, ready to flee on the instant, drew the eyes of the crowd. The party was more than ever desirous of holding the goodwill of the natives. They were about to leave their base, and the stores and petrol were absolutely at the mercy of these natives should they turn hostile. The desert party halted a few yards from the whites, who made friendly overtures. The natives, laughing away the young woman's fear, vehemently urged her forward. Dared by her own girl comrades she advanced fearfully, step by step, right up to Taylor.

Sutherland held out his hand, cooing as he would to a youngster: "Come along, Dickie Bird, shake hands with Pa-Pa."

She looked dubious, but chanced another step. Just then the camera fiend produced and levelled a camera. The lubra trembled but stood as if glued to the ground. Then she looked back towards her tribesmen and harangued them in a series of piercing shrieks. The tribesmen leaped up, their laughter turned to a fury of wild faces in an instant.

There rattled out the sharp "click! click! click! click!" of wommeras against spear hafts; their throwing arms, wrists and fingers clutched convulsively.

The whites, instantly alert, stood quietly waiting. Then the savages turned in a body and in a growing mob stamped rapidly away. The party watched with relief their expressive backs, the side glimpses of savage, excited faces, the waving of arms. What had so upset these temperamental savages they were not certain. Probably the superstitious fear of that "devilbox" the camera.

The morning came when all was packed and ready and they stood around to say farewell. As Blakeley shook hands with Lasseter his last words were:

"Harry, play safe! Take no risks. Remember we can always try some other way if you find you cannot get through on this trip. All the gold in Australia remember, is no good to you if you stay out there!"

Lasseter nodded grimly. Shaking hands with Taylor he said:

"Well, so long, Phil. If I don't find the reef I am never coming back!"

With slow, unconcerned stride the tiny camel team set out into the desert. The three men, with rather bitter thoughts, watched them merging into the sombre scenery. Those animals of the most ancient days were setting out to do what the most modern machines of man had failed to accomplish.

11. WHAT "THE STICK" MEANT

On the route to Alice Springs the truck party, at Taylor's Creek, said good-bye to Micky. That bashful Romeo wished to return to "Kitty". "She plurry good gin," he explained, with a blackfellow' s attempt at a blush.

"I don't think she's much of a wife," said Sutherland, in an aside to Blakeley. "Do you remember how skinny he was when he joined us."

"She makem plurry good damper," came back Micky, like a flash. "Not all a same a grindstone!"

They cheered Micky, and loaded him up with tucker to keep him fit on his sixty-mile walk to his beloved.

"He'd rather face his wife than the stick any day!" said Blakeley.

On arrival at Alice Springs Blakeley immediately wired the directors, stating his view of the position and asking instructions.

As the party would be some time in town, they seized the opportunity to unravel the mystery of the stick.

Blakeley picked out an aboriginal employed in town. He was one of these occasionally met with. Educated at one of the best South Australian schools, he had from a child practically lived with the whites. Blakeley arranged with this man to visit their quarters.

The men were prepared. The stick lay on the bed. When the aboriginal arrived he was greeted as a white man, as he was generally treated. Immediately he saw the stick his smile vanished. He gazed as if at something holy. He stepped towards the bed, his arms outspread, whispering. He crooned over the stick, but in a slightly different intonation to that which the men had already heard. Then he wheeled around with accusation in his eyes and demanded:

"How did you people come by this?"

"It was given us," answered Blakeley.

"By whom?"

Blakeley explained the circumstances, then added: "We are greatly puzzled. We would like to know all about the stick."

"Have any lubras seen it?"

"No, why?"

"Because it means death to any native woman who does. If word gets about of the presence of this stick, as you call it, every native will leave the town."

"That won't happen," broke in Taylor. "I'm sending the stick to Adelaide by the next train."

The man looked inexpressibly relieved.

"Now, won't you tell us what it all means?" asked Blakeley.

"I will fill in details," said the man slowly, "but no more. This stick is one of the sandhills gods. You people might best understand my meaning when I use the word 'god'. It bears the record, the life history of a tribe, from the time that tribe began. The spirits of many generations have breathed during the carving of that stick. It was stolen from the tribe whose history it records only a few years ago. A curse goes with the stealing of the god. The tribe from whom it was stolen must die out. The stick represents thousands of years of tribal history. In it is the spirit of the tribe, binding together all those men and women who have come and gone right from their first man and woman. When the stick is gone, the spiritual thread, you people would call it, of the tribe is broken; the tribe must die out. But" – and the interpreter stared at his listeners – "there is just one way, just one little chance in which the curse may be turned back upon the people who stole the stick. Should those people, the complete tribe down to the last piccaninny, be camped all together, and should there be a man of the lost tribe who has the right to wear the Kaditcha shoes, then, if he, wearing them, circles that tribe in the night they are lost!"

"By Jove," exclaimed Taylor, "those Kaditcha tracks Micky found. That's why the tribe were so scared."

"I'm beginning to see daylight now," said Blakeley, slowly.

"Wait a bit," drawled Sutherland, "I'll bet drinks all round we get it in the neck before he's finished."

"Go on," nodded Blakeley. "Your explanation is most interesting. But who wore those Kaditcha shoes?"

"You were showing Mr Carrington some photos yesterday," went on the man. "Do you remember them laughing at the funny little man in the old felt hat?"

"Rip Van Winkle!" exclaimed Taylor.

"This is he," said the narrator. "He may not appear very formidable; but when he wears the Kaditcha shoes his vicinity even is feared by the natives, perhaps more than a white man could fear anything. When he wears the shoes he is afraid of his own tracks! His body is above the earth, he is not of the earth. You white men could not understand how the shoes separate him from earth life. His is the tribe, the remains of the tribe, from whom the stick was stolen."

"Then the man who gave me the stick," asked Taylor, "was the actual thief?"

"He was."

"Then his tribe are now doomed, too?"

"They were!"

"But how have they got out of it?"

"By passing the curse on to you."

"Oh!"

"H'm!" added Blakeley.

"Huh!" grunted Sutherland.

"You see," explained the man, "they did what no other sandhills, nor any other tribe, have been able to do under similar circumstances. They gave the stick to you and you took it willingly. No natives in Australia, probably in the whole world, would have taken, willingly, that stick because in that way the curse passes on and the tribe who were circled by the Kaditcha shoes, goes free."

"They are still going," said Sutherland, reminiscently. The man made ready to leave.

"At that rate," said Blakeley slowly, "from the moment we took the stick, the curse began to work."

"Yes, your enterprise could never succeed." He turned as he opened the door. "Who actually laid his hands on the stick first?" he asked in a low voice.

"Lasseter," said Sutherland.

"He will never come back," said the man, and was gone.

"Phew!" whistled Taylor. "Didn't I tell you I had a wonderful curio!"

Sutherland laughed. "Better not let Lasseter get hold of it," he drawled, "or he'll chew old Rip Van's hoodoo up to bits."

"He won't," declared Taylor. "I'm packing it right away for Adelaide."

"It's a queer thing," mused Blakeley. "Of course, it's all nonsense to our way of thinking. But unwittingly we may have done a rather terrible thing in taking that god stick away. The natives believe in it, you know. It would be rather awful to think of those piccaninnies of old Rip Van's dying just because of it."

"But it's too late," said Sutherland. "The curse was finalized, so far as Rip Van's tribe was concerned, when the thing was first pinched. Think of those crippled kids of Rip Van's!"

To test the stick again, and to make sure the educated aboriginal was not pulling their legs, the men brought in two native men employed about the town. These entered the room with wide grins, expecting some lucrative job. But when they saw the stick they shrank back, their hands shielding their faces.

"What feller that one?" said Blakeley. "Him only stick, no hurt you."

But the two men retreated towards the door. "No show woman – she got die!" each mumbled, and left that room very frightened men.

"Cover that thing away," said Blakeley, "or we might have trouble over it. Officialdom might begin inquiries, and the officials have been very decent to us here."

"Come and have a drink," drawled Sutherland. "It's not every day we can get cursed by a native god!"

"It's not a god exactly," said Blakeley, thoughtfully, as they packed the stick away, "I've never even heard of any Australian natives having a real god. This thing goes far deeper. I can pretty well follow what that native meant, even though he left nearly everything unsaid. We've stumbled against something quite unknown to anthropologists, I believe. I wonder how Lasseter's getting on?"

"Are you coming for that drink?" drawled Sutherland, as he made towards the door.

12. THE FIGHT IN THE DESERT

The directors telegraphed instructions via Alice Springs that Coote and Taylor were to get in touch with Lasseter with all speed. Coote decided that Ayers Rock would prove a more suitable base than Ilbilba. The Rock was in a line with Lasseter's route, and natives said permanent water was there.

It was decided that Taylor should make all haste to form a base at Ayers Rock, taking out a camel team loaded with petrol and provisions. The party said good-bye to the Thornycroft with regret. That staunch friend of the last six months never failed in the roughest work. But it was due for a thorough overhaul and Taylor could not wait while it was entrained to and returned from Adelaide. He set busily to work hiring camels and equipment for the team. Immediately the base was established at Ayers Rock, Coote would try in a series of flights from the base to get in touch with Lasseter. These arrangements were completed, and Blakeley and Sutherland returned to Sydney.

Loaded camels with supplies and equipment leaving the base at Ayers Rock.

But it seemed as if the winds of the desert would hoodoo these machines of man. Suddenly a willy-willy shrieked upon Alice Springs, snapped the mooring ropes that held the party's 'plane, snatched it up, whirled it like a leaf in the air, then dashed it to the ground. Coote and Taylor came running, dismayed at the sight of the 'plane lurching like a wounded hornet upon its nose. Here was more delay, work, and expense. Taylor got on the job immediately. With the knowledge of Lasseter waiting, perhaps, for this 'plane, he worked night and day on the wrecked engine, mounting, removing the engine and completely rebuilding the nose of the machine.

Paddy Tucker, a half-caste camel driver, with his camels, was hired, the camels loaded with petrol and provisions, and Taylor started for Ayers Rock just as heavy seasonal rains came down.

Meanwhile, Lasseter had been steadily travelling in an unfamiliar land; a land of silences, of distances, of plain and desert and fertile lands, of great salt lakes, of canyoned ranges, of isolated mountains sitting in the midst of plains like monoliths of some prehistoric age.

Day after day the adventurers lurched on, the snake-like heads of the camels high in the air, the humped-up bodies of the riders swaying to the lurch of the long-legged beasts; the bull camel blathering and rumbling, always ready to give trouble, flapping his ridiculous tail and jerking back his vicious head to blow the air-bladder from his mouth in wrathy gurglings.

The two travelled away down past the Low Bluff Hills across to Petarde Spring and Mount Peculiar. Here they buried a hundred and fifty pounds of flour. It was obvious the camels were either unusually sulky or else overloaded; and a sulky camel is the most undependable beast in the world. The little camel was lagging behind and the big bull would persist in waiting for him. One day a family of natives, wild as the winds and as naked as at their birth, jumped up out of the grass beside them and insisted on accompanying them. Lasseter signified agreement with signs and odd words of the tongue he had picked up from Johns's natives. Here was another chance to learn a language of the Centralian tribes.

They mooched on to the far-flung shores of Lake Amadeus – that weird lake of salt. In a letter to his wife, Lasseter described its shores as a wonderful speedway. Its centre, however, was boggy. After pushing well out from the tree-lined shores, the camels refused to cross that glistening expanse. The ungainly beasts trembled at the knees; the big bull lurching round and roaring to escape back. The native guides walked out ahead, testing the salt crust. Then, each man leading a beast and with the little camel tied on behind, they coaxed and belted the brutes across fifteen hazardous miles. At times the camels broke through the crust and with bestial screamings sank slowly into the thick blue mud, while the men rushed with shrubs to pack under their labouring knees and pads.

Once past the lake, they travelled past large patches of white gum and casuarina and well grassed flats on into a maze of barren sandhills, then into flat country and spinifex and mulga. Presently, far away, like a black domed pyramid above a sea of saltbush, wattle and mulga, rose the mighty ramparts of Mount Olga.

They camped beside this pyramid of nature. It was like an old-time city of domed temples piled one upon the other. Several temples were eight hundred feet in height. The whole mass is two miles long by three-quarters of a mile broad. Within its moaning labyrinths owls nest, also hawks and desert birds; they echo to the hoot of the rock pigeon and the solemn call of the mopoke. It is the aborigines' "Katatuta". They swear it is the home of Spirit People and the dwelling-place of souls who seek life again upon this vale of woe.

The party crossed a desert strip, finding water at Murra Thurra, the salt lagoon; then wandered up valleys between mountains where quartzite blended with ironstone. Here, their native acquaintances disappeared in the night as silently as they had come. But Lasseter had learned quite a lot.

Often, near and far, the thin coiling smokes of the myalls signalled the invaders' approach. At night the men were very wary; seeing that the fire never blazed; sitting there quietly talking, eyes and ears alert, listening for a sound of stealthy approach.

One quiet evening Lasseter and Johns were camped in a gorge walled in by gloomy rocks. The only sounds were their low-toned conversation and a sighing that may have been the wind in some rock-walled ravine. Had a pterodactyl swooped down from those old-time crags, it would hardly have been out of place. Suddenly the gorge roared and echoed in answering roar with a snarling scream and clash of animal teeth. The men's hair stood on end. They snatched up guns as their camels rose grunting; they ran to quieten the beasts. From the gorge came a furious scrambling, the lurch and slip and slide of two great bodies. Two wild bull camels were fighting over a lady friend! The men quietened their own uneasy brutes with the angry remonstrance that comes from relief. They had had quite a scare.

In a rock cleft near by a tiny reservoir of fresh water was found craftily hidden under a flat stone. Treasured possession of some unnamed tribe, the whites would fare ill should they be taken by surprise. Lasseter smiled at times at the jealousy of the natives over their puny hidden soaks. Why, when the white man came he would make the rivers flow again; he would cover the land with wells and lakes in the form of station tanks; he would make many blades of grass grow where one grew now.

Paul Johns, youth and wanderer, was intensely interested in this trip. He was excited at the quest for this great gold reef, discussed wherever men congregate in Centralia. Lasseter liked the man.

They went on until Lasseter picked up a landmark he recognized. Then in long stages they began crossing and recrossing in efforts to pick up the auriferous section in which long ago he had located the reef. They travelled by soaks, sometimes three and four days apart. And yet this country was not all desert by any means. There were areas of good grass, areas of nutritive saltbush, areas of the queer parakelia grass. Lasseter recognized quite a number of trees and shrubs whose foliage in drought would be eagerly eaten by stock. He knew, too, that hundreds of miles farther to the north-west stockmen were pushing out into similar country, having found that the despised "desert" grasses could be and were eaten by stock.

Once, when travelling across particularly barren country, there came a shrill whistle as, in a whirlwind of hoofs, a brumby mob tore down upon them. Bursting from the bushes they wheeled around the men, pawing the earth in snorting hostility. The camels kept straight on, unresponsive, unperturbed. Lasseter gazed on the sleekness of these wild horses' coats, on their good condition, their physical fitness. And, to his knowledge, the nearest water was three long camel rides away. The secret was in the parakelia grass. In appearance something like ice-plant, its thick leaves were stored with water. The wild camels and horses live in the sand-ridges for unbelievable periods on this worthless-looking but highly nutritive grass.

Lasseter, swaying hour after hour, day after day, on his camel, dreamed dreams and saw visions of the findings of his gold reef and of the subsequent rush. He dreamed, too, of boring for artesian water which would make this desert blossom into a great new State for Australia.

The men camped early one afternoon among hills dotted with quandong trees, those rich scarlet plums of the desert. Johns had gone away with the gun; there were wallabies in the caves. Lasseter sat with his back to the packsaddle, a scribbling pad upon his knee, a smile upon his face. He was writing to "Bobbie". A rifle shot rang out. Lasseter sighed. A moment later he looked up at a visitor, a baby emu, trustfully approaching, its young feathers brown and black striped, its bright, wide awake eyes trying to tell him something. Lasseter described the baby to Bobbie; then put down his pad and tried to shoo him away before Johns came back with the gun. He had quite a lot of trouble getting rid of him and had to finish his letter by firelight.

Once again, a family of myalls stepped from the grass and joined in behind the camels. The "old man", his matted hair tied round with emu feathers into a chignon, with a lordly air, carried his spears. His wife carried a smile and a baby straddling each hip. The five other "steps and stairs" carried the household utensils and an appreciable amount of dirt. Their big round eyes stared up at the camels as if they were the mountains of Mahomet.

Lasseter was not deceived by the childlike innocence of these self-appointed guides. He knew their job was to lure him away from waterholes; he knew they were spies for the tribe. But he liked those little wild children.

Ever searching, they meandered into a fairy glen of trickling water and palms that would have graced a coral strand. In that trip they left their camel-pads in more than one such glen – beautiful oases of water and grass and palms looking like survivals of some forgotten age before the desert began.

The two men crossed the desert once more – a dreadful dash of seven days between waterholes. Then came the tail-end of a monsoonal rain. Lasseter was staggered at that rain; he worked one pouring afternoon in building an earth-work around the camp to prevent the stores being washed away! When camp was struck, the camels bogged! They struggled desperately on. Lasseter had recognized his country! The men turned into it and a wild light came into Lasseter's eyes. He laughed each time a camel sank down, and he laughed as they strained and pulled and struggled to get the beast on to its clumsy feet again. So sure on sand, so clumsy in bog! To think that all these months the desert had stopped him from reaching his heart's desire and, now that he had almost done so, there came rain and bog!

Johns worked with the gold-fever in his veins and urged the camels on. When they got to within twenty miles of the reef they landed the camels in an impassable morass hemmed in on the far distant side by barriers of rocks. Lasseter struggled on alone, on foot, to make sure. When he returned he repeatedly looked up at the sky, smiling as he watched and listened. Johns eagerly questioned Lasseter. He wanted to know – too much!

It may have been the strain; it may have been suspicion and distrust; while sitting sullenly at a meal Johns called Lasseter a liar. Lasseter threw his plate of food in the other's face and they fought like fiends. One drew his revolver, but the other grabbed his wrist. They fought to their knees for that gun. The hammer jarred down between Lasseter's left finger and thumb. In pain, he wrenched his wrist free and hurled the revolver into the spinifex. They sprang up, panting, mad-eyed, each awaiting the other's rush. For minutes they glared, then turned and with shaking limbs started packing the camels for the forced return trip.

Back at Ilbilba, Lasseter dispatched Johns to Alice Springs with a letter to the Government Resident. After delivering the letter Johns was to return to Ilbilba with a bushman friend of Lasseter's, named Johannsen, and remove the food dump to Lake Christopher, over the Western Australian border. By Johns, Lasseter also sent a letter and a telegram to the directors of the Company, explaining his trip, stating that he was going straight out again, giving directions as to the route he would take, and how he was to be followed and located.

Johns faithfully carried out his instructions. Lasseter, with two camels, set off alone on his last ride.

13. THE HOODOO

Taylor, after leaving Alice Springs, was immediately in difficulties. Every parched watercourse ran a banker; the Finke River in swirling brown flood carried the reviver of life right down through Central Australia.

The camels, blubbering and snarling their freshness, put their heads to the ground and shook their packs like a dog shaking off fleas. Straps were broken, cases went flying, bags of foodstuffs littered the ground as the camels bolted. In mad abandon they sped away, saddles slipping and swaying under their bellies until flung trampled to the ground.

The exhausted men travelled only seven miles from Alice Springs that day. Most of their camels had "gone bush". Paddy Tucker, the camel driver, furious and almost collapsing, stretched out by the camp-fire, refusing to go another yard unless he had the further assistance of at least a black boy. Taylor returned to Alice Springs. He secured a boy who uncompromisingly demanded high wages and luxurious conditions. Taylor made a desperate bargain and hurried back to the camels. The black boy deserted in the night. Taylor returned to the Springs and the police yanked a heathen native out of gaol and signed him to the service of Taylor, who returned to the job dubious of his auxiliary help. The snarling brutes of the desert were tracked, secured, loaded, and the team mooched on into the threatening west.

Coote set out from Alice Springs on a quick six-hundred-mile flight. He landed at Hermannsburg Mission, eighty miles west of the Springs and two hundred south-west of Ilbilba. This outpost in Centralia made him welcome. Superintendent Albrecht readily sent out a black tracker with a Petermann Range myall native to search for Lasseter. They were to cut the prospector's tracks if possible and follow him up with a letter telling him of the change of base, and deliver letters of instruction from the directors. Coote resumed his flight, circling Butler's Dome and the hundreds of miles of country upon which he thought he might see Lasseter or his signal fires; then he circled Ilbilba and saw not a soul there. He returned to Alice Springs and hurriedly made preparations for his flight to Ayers Rock to link up with Taylor.

Taylor was pushing on into most unexpected trouble. Large areas of the country were boggy after the rains, and in these the big-footed camels went down, snarling like helpless mammoths. The three men, crawling about the hapless beasts like ants around a bogged snail, had again and again to unpack the loads before the camels could lurch out of the mire.

Taylor was going to be late. Anxiously he tried to get round the boggy country, seeking the hard ground. The days slipped by; he travelled as far into the evening as his camels would allow.

Before leaving for Ayers Creek, Coote arranged with the Government Resident, Mr Carrington, to send out a search party should he and Taylor not return before the end of November.

The airman commenced his flight on a clear day, but with a heat that at a thousand feet up seemed to catch the breath. This "thin" air caused violent atmospheric conditions. At times the *Golden Quest II* roared sideways as if to hurtle through space, then heaved over, anxious to dash straight to the ground.

When approaching the Hermannsburg Mission the *Quest* sped into a fiery sky of rainbows where the sun pierced a pall of fine red dust. Coote landed at the mission rather gladly. Flying through a dust haze is risky. He was welcomed and pressed to stay the night. Next morning Mrs Heinrich insisted that he load up with eggs, cabbages, carrots, and a bottle of beef-malt wine. Coote laughingly accepted all, little knowing how he was to appreciate the gift in the near future. On leaving, Superintendent Albrecht suggested that, in view of the dangerous nature of the country, Coote should return on the following Saturday, bringing news of himself and Taylor. The mission, being equipped with wireless, could then acquaint civilization that the party was safely established at the Rock.

Coote agreed and took to the air light-heartedly, flying a compass course over forty miles of mountain peaks lying like monstrous brown waves far below; then over a sandhills country that faded into distance. A dozen times he dodged willy-willies that spiralled up from the earth as whirling columns of sand spinning across flat country and snatching up dried bushes and leaves. But he was more concerned about those whirlwinds of air he could not see.

Away to the left appeared the little bunch of knobs that were bold Mount Olga. Hazily to the right rose table-topped Mount Connor. Straight ahead, rapidly looming up like a turreted battleship out of a misty red haze, was Ayers Rock. Coote circled round and round this Gibraltar of the desert, his engine roaring. The Rock faces were gleaming under the sunlight where water seeped over from the summit. He circled as a hawk would skim mountain cliffs. Where was the landing-ground? Coote stared down at a sea of shrubbery with no sign of a man.

A gale had sprung up; the 'plane lurched violently. Thinking Taylor might have mistaken Mount Connor for Ayers Rock, Coote set off on the twenty-miles dash, the 'plane taking its buffetings in a series of plunges. He circled the ramparts but saw no living thing. Then he turned back for the Rock and the waterholes he had seen there. Again he circled it, in ever widening circles, seeking a landing-ground. Finally there shone up at him a sand patch covered with porcupine grass framed with mulga trees. Manoeuvring against the duckings of the 'plane he saw there was a chance of sufficient room to take off again, so, flying against the wind, he settled down to land, dodging a clump of bushes as he touched. The machine slid along without even sinking into the ground, but his gleeful laugh was cut short when a sharp report sent a splinter of wood whizzing past the machine. With a deep premonition he climbed from the cockpit and found the blade splintered and a section of metal casing lifted out. The damage, though comparatively slight, was quite sufficient to stop the flight of the machine until repaired.

Coote roped the 'plane securely to the ground, fearful lest a willy-willy whirl it among the trees. Then he walked away towards the Rock. A whirring flock of doves from the grass startled him. He listened, but there came no grunt of camel, no tinkle of bell, no song from a camp. Only a brooding silence! He walked two miles, cautiously edging through the mulga when he neared the Rock, for he knew this was an aborigines' sacred camping-ground and some of the tribes who corroboreed there were notoriously hostile to whites.

But there was neither white man nor black. Coote stared apprehensively at gloomy black clefts in the huge rock wall. He ventured on the little grassy plains that, like trimmed lawns, run round the base of the rock; then skirted the big waterholes, searching for some sign of man. There was only silence and a lone camel track going out into the desert.

Where was Taylor? What had happened to him? Was he lost? Had he had trouble with natives? In a maze of uncertainty Coote returned to the 'plane and had something to eat. Then he sat listening far into the night, staring over the mulga tops at the ghostly wall of rock, searching its mistiness for any reflection of a fire.

Coote scraped a hole in the sand behind his machine and coiled up in it, seeking warmth. At dawn he shivered as he crawled from the hole, shook the sand from his clothes, and ate a thoughtful breakfast. He took a pot of red paint from the 'plane and set off for the Rock, completely circling it throughout the day and painting S.O.S. notices on it by each waterhole, giving his position and date of landing. Dog tired, he returned to the 'plane that evening and settled down for a long wait. Slowly eating a meagre ration of food, he reasoned that the Hermannsburg people would not be able to reach him under three weeks with camels. He blessed the forethought of Mrs Heinrich.

Coote determined to stay by the 'plane until his water gave out, lest hostile myalls trap him at the rock-hole. The mulga screened the 'plane here and – a 'plane leaves no tracks.

He waited there another six long days, until reduced to his last pint of water. Where could Taylor be? Where was Lasseter? Coote swore loudly, staring at the 'plane, wondering what was the hoodoo this country had put on the expedition.

Next day he rolled his swag and, packing the food that remained, set out for the Rock, carrying his swag in relays. Great shadows from the Rock cloaked the plain before he neared the big waterhole at the north-eastern corner. Very thirsty, he dumped his swag and almost ran through the gloom – to stand abruptly as he rounded a buttress of rock and saw three bright fires, with another being lit away to the right. He stood as still as the rock, listening. No sight of humans, no sound of voices, no sound of camels! It must be a party of myalls in for a sacred corroboree. Coote crept away. If the wild men were intent on their sacred ceremonies it was a scene on which a lone white man dare not intrude.

At daylight his thirst was unbearable. Drawing his revolver, he crept to the rock spur and sidled along it. He rounded the spur – and was dumbfounded to see camel packs and a white man stooping over a fire. Taylor sprang up in amazement.

"Where the devil did you spring from?" he yelled.

"Where the devil have you been?" replied Coote, as he dashed for the billy of tea.

14. LASSETER'S LAST RIDE: ELDORADO FOUND

Lasseter rode happily away on his last journey. He felt master of the situation now. Disappointing experiences had undermined his faith in modern transport, its boasted speed and surety. As he travelled, he mused on the curious slipping back of the expedition's transport; right back now to camels and man. What memories this land must have, could it only speak! Strange, how he felt part of it! Quite uncanny, this surety that he was of this land and always would be: it had drawn him back again after thirty years. After all, he felt a warm satisfaction in going out alone to find his reef. Alone he had found it first; again he would find it alone. And then –?

Lasseter gazed up at the clear blue sky. Out of it would come aeroplanes. That was where modern transport would come into its own, when the path-finders' job was done. Then would come the rush, the opening up of a goldfield, the settlement of a new State. A native, rising Phoenix-like from the land, watched him as he passed.

Each sundown he picked carefully his camping-ground, never camping where natives might creep on him unobserved and unheard. He slept lightly, alert at the rustle of a twig, and he was always awake before dawn. That was the most dangerous time. A hundred miles from Ilbilba he saw the first smoke spiral ascending; another from a distant ridge answered. Myall natives were signalling the lone rider's approach. In late afternoon he watched two crows, flying low, going to water. He would watch for their early morning flight, for they camp near water.

That evening Lasseter hobbled his camels without bells, lit a fire, and ate his solitary meal. A mopoke croaked dismally. As the fire burned down to coals the man became shadowed just out of the glow. Around him settled the desert silence; above, a dome of velvet black blazed with stars. The air was sweet and cool. At stealthy steps behind him Lasseter turned, revolver in hand. A camel grunted restively, answered harshly by its mate. The brutes, without reason, were becoming more bad-tempered day by day. He threw some twigs on the coals and in the light of their blaze spread his blankets and turned in. As the twigs burned down the shape of the sleeper merged with the night.

But Lasseter was stealthily piling up sand alongside his body nearest the fire. He drew one blanket over the body-like mound, then, pushing the other before him, crawled fifty yards into the deepest shadows. He slept well, not caring much even should a shower of spears fly into that mound by the fire. And so he slept on other lonely nights.

Next afternoon, black figures abruptly crested a hill in front. In menacing array they rattled spears, brandished arms, and leaped with a piercing chorus to stamp the ground in savage rhythm.

In readiness for, but dreading a fight, Lasseter kept on, his camels never deviating as they lurched along the foot of the hill. He knew that if he turned aside they would never let him return again. But a fight meant that if he won out the natives would dog him for days, unseen, tireless, deadly enemies. Hopefully, he recognized they were only a hunting party. Had they flaunted the ochred feathers of a fighting party, his position would have been serious indeed. He stared steadily up as he rode along, hand on revolver, watching those poised spears now settled down into the wommeras, ready to fire the instant a spear arm was jerked for the throw. But he passed and jeering voices grew fainter. Looking back, he saw the natives grouped on the hilltop like black statues against the sunset.

Thereafter they watched him daily all the way to Winter's Glen. Twice they rose from the bushes almost within spear throw. Should he find one of their hidden soaks, or unwittingly camp on one of their sacred grounds, there would be a fight.

Though the surface water had dried up, much of the country was beautiful after the rains. Acacia and quandong trees, Mitchell and kangaroo grasses were abundant. Some shrubs were in flower, and grass parrots were noisy among the seeds. While in the sandhills country, he rode past one red hill vivid with scarlet flowers. Occasionally, a desert bush was a yellow glory of trailing vines. His fat camels one day waded across a plain knee-deep in luscious grass, and Lasseter dreamed again of a goldfields stampede and artesian water and this country under sheep and wheat. This country was not the desert proper, with its leagues of barren sand, but part of the great "desert fringe" – desert mainly through lack of water. He yelled like a boy one day at the sight of rabbits. The white-tailed little beasts were as great wanderers as himself. Fancy them making their way right out here! How the desert men must welcome them!

At Winter's Glen he spelled his camels. Later on, he hoped to meet Johns and Johannsen at Lake Christopher, eighty miles west of the Glen. He often wondered how the directors had taken the break-up of the expedition. He had a conviction they would seek him by aeroplane, although they were under no obligation to do so. Lasseter travelled on to the Western Australian border, skirting the edge of the true desert. His heart sang as he recognized landmark after landmark. He had seen no sign of natives since leaving the Glen. Now he suddenly became aware of unseen presences watching and following him. He gazed all around at sombre rocky hills, between which were plains of sand dotted by clumps of desert bush. There was not a sign of native, in person or by "talk" smoke.

But this sixth sense developed on former trips was sharpening since the desert had again taken Lasseter to its heart. He knew natives were there. One morning he crept from his retreat to light the fire and found men's tracks in the ashes. This was "another" country, inhabited by a different tribe. Uneasily he wondered what their methods would be. He urged his camels away from that clump of gidgee on ahead. He swore at the camels, jerking the brutes in the direction he wanted them to take. They lifted high their heads and roared out across the desert, slathering the sands with foam. The brutes for some inexplicable reason were becoming almost unmanageable.

Lasseter found his reef. As he gazed upon it, a feeling came over him that he had done his life's work. He sat down by the greenish-white quartz, staring across the hill where the reef outcropped like a yellowish-brown cap, and for two hours never moved. These blobs of dull yellow in this quartz had been the magnet drawing his thoughts for thirty years. This reef, he felt, was his life. He stood erect, with a long sigh, staring at the tallest of the hills, fixing them indelibly in his mind. He would peg the reef, then return to the nearest soak he knew of, more than a day's travel away, then scout out towards Lake Christopher and wait for Johns and Johannsen with supplies. How he wished now that the *Golden Quest* was coming, to hurry back to civilization with the news! He felt that his mates were coming. Taylor had been his best chum; he felt sure Taylor was coming. If the Company could only see him now!

He knapped off some of the stone. His heart beat violently at the sight of the yellow gleaming in the fractured rock. The reef was phenomenally rich: some of the stone was actually held together by threads of gold. Laughing aloud, he held up a gleaming specimen! It thrilled him. How it glistened! That yellow stuff that could make a man a king! Where was Harding now? In the heat of his delight he stared soberly around, sensing that his long-dead surveyor mate was with him. Quietly he filled a bag with specimens.

There was no water near the reef, but the camels carried sufficient to last him out. He hobbled the camels and by sundown had cut the pegs and driven in the datum peg. The rest took much longer. It was two days before he had pegged the reef and recorded the necessary observations. In the letter describing the location he wrote, among other things: "I am afraid the natives will pull up the pegs after I have gone, for the reef is upon one of their sacred grounds. However, I have written upon the posts and photographed them and will bury the evidences of truth, with a bag of specimens, under the camp-fire ashes."

In that manner Lasseter usually buried letters, so that members of the party could follow him up. He knew the natives would scratch up anything they believed he had buried. But letters in a tin buried under a camp-fire would be the safest place. The keenest eyes could detect no sign of anything buried underneath a little heap of still-warm ashes.

It had been a hard day and the camels were savage, expecting water. Tomorrow they must have it, though the bad-tempered brutes could go without for another day if necessary. Lasseter started off in the afternoon, seeking to make the most of nearly three hours of daylight left. The camels travelled swiftly. The brutes always know when they are travelling back to water. The sun set in a fiery glow that made the Western Australian desert cruelly beautiful. Those rolling leagues of barren sand appeared a sea of softest pink set in a dreadful silence. Lasseter urged his beasts to earth on a clear patch of sand between low hills fringed by desert bush. There was little chance of natives successfully sneaking on him here. As he stooped over the kneeling brutes he spoke to them, "Ssh! Ssh!" as he began to unload, crooning a quietness to their snarling grunts. He turned to dump a bag of foodstuffs upon the ground. A swishing of the sand, a creaking lurch, wheeled him swiftly. The camels were almost to their feet. As he shouted and ran they were up on their knees, and as he sprang at the rump of the nearest he was flung violently on to the sand and they were away. He sprang up and grabbed a nosepeg. The camel bellowed and swung him high, with a vicious shake of the head that sent Lasseter flying. He jumped up again and raced after them, shrieking, the nosepeg in his hand. A bolting camel travels at an amazing speed. These beasts, gone "macnoon", covered the ground in giant strides, frothily bellowing. With the terrific shaking the water-tin lid flew loose and sprays of priceless fluid rained out on the desert sand.

Lasseter went "macnoon", too. He drew his revolver and fired again and again. He fired to kill the camel and save his water – his life. But the camels sped into the distance, disappearing among stunted bush, appearing again on the sands, disappearing and reappearing until they faded like gigantic spiders into the ribboned sunset. They would travel, fifty, eighty, a hundred miles or more without stopping.

Lasseter was alone in the desert without water; with food perhaps for a fortnight. His food! What if the blacks were robbing the only thing now that was his! Anxiously he started back on his tracks. He had a long way to go. His footsteps slowed as in the twilight he saw the bag of food lying on the sand. He stood by the bag and listened. What a silence! Shadows stood straight up out of the sands. Lasseter's heart thumped as he whipped out his revolver and faced those desert men.

15. THIRST

At Ayers Rock Taylor did an excellent repair job to the 'plane, mending the propeller mostly with strips of petrol tin.

"It will take you to Alice Springs," he guaranteed Coote. "But if you attempt the flight to Adelaide the vibration will shatter the blade."

Paddy Tucker, whose contract was ended, was sent back to Alice Springs. Taylor retained Jacky and two camels which had been lent him by Bob Buck. He would stay by the Rock and prepare an aerodrome. Coote would fly the 'plane back to Alice Springs, attempt to fly it to Adelaide for repairs, and return with it as soon as possible.

Coote set off for Alice Springs, rising up fast and almost immediately disappearing into a dust haze. At Alice Springs he found he had caused nation-wide concern. The Hermannsburg Mission had wired the Company that he was some days overdue. Search parties had, days ago, set out from the mission. Three Defence 'planes, at the instigation of the Company, had been dispatched under Flight-Lieutenant Eaton that very day from Melbourne. Kingsford Smith and other airmen held their 'planes in readiness. Coote immediately telegraphed the directors that he had arrived. Anxiety on his account off their minds, the directors at once set about formulating plans to get in touch with Lasseter.

Taylor, with Jacky, after Coote's departure, set busily to work clearing a 'drome right against the Rock. Taylor was never tired of admiring it. That stupendous rock, a mile across its domed top, two miles long, and towering a thousand feet above the plain, would not be denied admiration. Taylor would gaze at the caves far up in its face. Some of those caves are large enough to hold a church. Grotesque paintings of men, women, and animals adorn their red walls, and bones from aborigines' feasts litter the floors. Gloomy little caves up near the summit are shared by bats and wee striped birds.

This Rock is the "Uluru" of the natives, the most sacred spot in all Centralia. It is the birthplace of many of their traditions, the home of the Spirit folk. Large sections of the Rock are so sacred that women are not allowed in such vicinities. Death is the penalty for transgression. Jacky proudly showed Taylor "a secret". He smiled in the shadowed end of a rock gallery and whispered. His speech came trilling away to Taylor at the other end in whispered perfect words.

They built a bough-shed camp near the large waterhole on a lawn of couch grass that would have graced a Sydney garden. Their fire was built down-wind and banked up every morning with ashes, because of the dreaded willy-willies. Taylor could appreciate the beliefs of the natives that an evil spirit lurks in each whirling wind fiend. Day by day the work progressed. One Wednesday morning they awoke to find that a camel had cleared out during the night. Jacky followed his tracks some miles, but returned without him.

"That damn camel thirty miles away now. He go all a way back longa Bob Buck's station."

"Well, let him go then," said Taylor. "He's making for home anyway and we would never catch him."

That evening they returned to camp very tired. Jacky saw it first but checked his alarm. Taylor stared around uncomprehending then exclaimed: "My God!"

The camp was a heap of ashes. Jacky traced the course of the willy-willy that had scooped up the camp-fire cinders, whirling the gleaming embers into the dry bough shed. It had brought this ruin against the wind. Majestic shadow enveloped them as they scraped amongst the ashes for scraps of food. Records, the company's belongings, personal belongings, a thousand photos, lay in those white ashes.

Action was imperative. Alice Springs was a fortnight's camel ride away. But Bob Buck's Tempe Downs Station was only four days.

"Jacky," ordered Taylor, "you clean out that oil drum and fill it with water ready to load on the camel. Scrub it out well with sand now. I'll rake these ashes for anything I can find and we'll start at sun up."

That night, he made a little bag out of a piece of burnt tarpaulin. The rising sun turned the dome of the Rock to burnished gold. Taylor in fancy had often likened that gold to the golden sheets on some old-time temple. This morning he apprehensively turned his back on the dawning splendour, recognizing in it the coming heat of an awful day.

Taking it in turns to ride the camel, the two men travelled over red sandhills with the temperature a 120 degrees in the shade. Strangely enough, Jacky's feet got frightfully sore. For years he had worked for white men and had often worn their boots. His had been burned in the fire and now his feet wouldn't stand those burning sands. They had only one day's food. There was about one day's water in the water-bag. On the second evening Taylor opened the water drum. He dipped in a pannikin and raised it thirstily to his lips and gulped. His face blanched. Like a stricken man he stared out into the desert. The water, pungent with chemicals, was black and scummy and oily!

Jacky had cleaned the tin. Yes, faithfully he had scrubbed it well with sand. He was a civilized boy and had cleaned many a pannikin and billycan. But what did he understand about aeroplane oils and chemicals and the thorough boiling of an oil drum!

"Oh, Jacky, Jacky!" wailed Taylor. "Why didn't I do it myself!"

He emptied the drum lest his thirst force him to drink the poison. The sun rose like molten iron, eating up the long shadow of the striding camel. Taylor had to force the heart-broken Jacky to take his turn at riding the beast. Before midday, the thirst was awful. Taylor's tongue was swelling; his eyes were bloodshot. He gazed around for a shady bush.

"Me think it better we push on, Boss," said Jacky, urgently. "Chew him stone."

They did push on, right into a desert of red iron-sand, with the setting sun like blood. Before dawn Jacky helped Taylor on to the camel, then led it. He refused to ride at all. In early morning Taylor was swaying clutching the saddle. Suddenly he stiffened with a stabbing pain in the small of his back. In agonized remembrance he recalled an old kidney operation of years back.

Before midday he was delirious. Jacky tried both to guide the camel and keep Taylor from falling off. A taller bush stood up out of pure red sand. Jacky made for it, his bleeding feet clogged with burning sand. He forced the camel to kneel, and as it lurched to its knees he snatched at the sick man and lifted him off, laying him down with his head and shoulders in the shade. It was a pitiable shade, but it was the best. The remainder of that day he bent over Taylor, fanning the flies from him, feeling his forehead with rough black hands, trying to keep him cool.

At sundown he shook the moans from Taylor's lips. "We move now, Boss," he insisted urgently. "We ride on. Suppose we stop tonight you never move another day!"

He lifted Taylor to the camel, roped him on, knotted his ankles to the saddle, and tied his wrists and his body. The camel lurched up, not unwillingly. Jacky steadied the human bundle against the upward jolt; then, taking the leading rope, set out with long even strides.

Through a silent night, under piercing stars, in a terrible stillness accentuated by the "whouf, whouf" of the camel's pads, they pressed on. A camel and man travel a wonderful distance throughout a night from sunset to dawn. But a blazing sun had made tinder-dry the rough homestead of Tempe Downs Station before Jacky came over the horizon, his eyes blood red, his thick purple lips blistered and gasping.

Bob Buck nursed Taylor back to life, then to partial strength. When he had recovered sufficiently to travel, Buck fitted him out with camels and black boys to take him to Hermannsburg Mission. Here Taylor wirelessed Alice Springs, instructing Coote to fly to Hermannsburg. Alice Springs replied that Coote had returned to Sydney. Taylor then telegraphed the directors, telling them of his misfortune, and asking for instructions.

The fresh vegetables grown at the Mission, helped by a woman's care, built Taylor up considerably, and soon he headed his camels for Alice Springs. There he had to receive medical attention for kidney trouble and for his eyes, which had been affected by heat and sand. Johns had arrived with Lasseter's letters. The directors telegraphed Taylor to hold Johns and proceed with all speed to Ilbilba, there to refit the base and do all in his power to get in touch with Lasseter. He was also to be prepared for the arrival of the reconditioned 'plane with Captain Pittendrigh and mining engineer Hamre, who were being sent to assist in the search and the repegging of the reef.

Lasseter with the plane *Golden Quest II* after the accident.

Taylor set to work joyfully to carry out his fresh instructions. Lasseter was somewhere out there – waiting. Taylor hired a camel team from Bob Buck and he and Johns set about the loading.

Meanwhile, several camel-team prospecting parties had come in from somewhere out in the Petermann Ranges. News had got about the town that Lasseter had located his reef. It was whispered to Taylor that the prospectors were going to track him out and be in on the find.

Taylor was perturbed. The Company appeared to be within an ace of success. To have, perhaps, the pick of the gold snatched from the shareholders at this last moment, was heartbreaking. Then he suddenly remembered the 'plane and smiled grimly. Even natives cannot track a 'plane.

The camel team set off for Ilbilba via the Hermannsburg Mission. This isolated outpost, which now had come so prominently into the lives of the party, was a place of great interest to Taylor. On the fringe of the desert it holds nine hundred square miles of cattle country. Within its widespread domains, and fifteen miles south of the Mission, is the beautiful Glen of Palms, an Eden in the "dead heart" of Australia. There are the oldest palms known in the world, silver waterfalls hidden by ferns, singing birds, limpid pools alive with small, queerly marked fish, groves of the towering Mariae palm (the only ones of their species in Australia) and grottoes draped with clinging vines, the beauty of which almost takes one's breath away. But even here there brooded that waiting silence. And here and there, too, beside a slab of rock or under a creeper-covered mound, were graves of wanderers who had fallen to the spears of the blacks.

It was here that the A.I.M. had installed one of their unique "Baby" Receiving and Transmitting sets with the object of doing their bit towards the pioneering of the country.

Taylor and Johns, in ten long days travel from Hermannsburg, reached Ilbilba. Taylor immediately recognized some of his old native friends. Eagerly he inquired for news of Lasseter. But they shook their heads. Then he asked of a "great bird". Again they shook their heads.

He set the natives to piling up dry bushes in readiness for smoke signals to the 'plane.

16. BARGAINING FOR LIFE

Lasseter beckoned the natives towards him, cheerily calling in desert lingo, "Those damn kamellie in a hurry! Come to my fire: we are friends."

He prayed they understood him. He could see no lubras: an ominous sign. The wild men did not move. Lasseter commenced rooting around a bush for sticks. He knelt to make a fire, but tensely alert.

The tallest man stepped noiselessly forward. Lasseter was erect and waiting as the savage came right up to him, truculent and menacing. Lasseter gripped the man's hand and shook it, feeling the fingers under his clench hard on the spear haft. The man was surprised. His strong teeth showed white in his wide black mouth. His coarse hair was drawn back from the forehead by a band of animal fur in which was flaunted a solitary eagle feather.

Lasseter spoke again. But the man refused to talk – his brow lowering, his eyes glaring unwaveringly. The hair on his chest would have made a mat. His back and muscular shoulders were all ridged by the cicatrized weals of warriorhood.

Lasseter took a desperate chance. He stared the savage in the eyes, pulled out his revolver, twirled the cylinder to quick clickings, pointed the muzzle at the man, and struck him lightly on the stomach. He held his breath, ready to fire. But the startled glare in those rolling eyes told him that the savage understood.

Lasseter sheathed his weapon. How he wished he had shot the camel! What an impression it would have made! Whistling a jazz tune, he undid the bag of foodstuffs. With mysterious ceremony he spread the contents out one by one, seeking to divert their interest. Those shadowy forms were creeping closer. He invited the man to join him in a meal. As if this were something all could understand and appreciate, he found himself noiselessly surrounded by men. How their eyes gleamed! All had big scars on their abdomens. The younger men especially had blistered sores there, caused by warming themselves with firesticks. He nodded at the hungry circle and waved them to sit. They squatted, all but the savage chief. His ominous frown Lasseter pretended not to notice. The greasy smell from the naked bodies put him in mind of a lion's den. A big firefly glowed out in the night, then vanished.

"A firestick," thought Lasseter. "The lubras must be crouching out there."

He asked for water. A man called softly, and in answer other shadows closed in: lubras and children, tousle-haired and intensely curious. Numbers of the children had dreadful scars on their bodies, caused by rolling in the fire when asleep. Lasseter could actually feel the stare from sixty pairs of eyes, the sense of high-pitched hesitancy awaiting the moment to dash in and kill.

In little canoe-shaped pitchis of wood some women carried native foods, while others, sure of foot, carried upon their heads precious pitchis of water. The young ones stared and giggled at Lasseter as if he were a man from Mars. Several of these beauties were so red-ochred that their bodies appeared to have red skins, a not unpleasing effect with their wild black eyes shining below a rattling fringe of bloodwood seeds. Some had hair falling to the shoulders, the ends tufted with fluffs of wallaby fur. Lasseter put the billy on and threw kindling on the fire, but the chief, with a guttural curse, stamped his huge foot on the blaze. Lasseter expostulated, taking care that his meaning was understood by all the crowd. He must have fire to make food. Low growls told that some sided with him. They were intensely curious as to what he was going to do. These people had never seen a billy boiled. They stared at the articles strewn around. They thought the treacle tin was wonderful. All were mysterious things to them – probably things of evil. But some things were food, and they understood so well the craving for food. If they killed this man now, as Watta Mitta Mitta urged, they would not know which of the things was safe to eat.

Lasseter rekindled the fire, taking care it was but a blaze sufficient to boil the billy. These people loved fire; it was their friend, their companion. But they had an inherited dread of a blaze that might betray them to enemies.

He sugared the tea honey-sweet, knowing how fond aborigines are of sweet things, poured out a pannikin with ceremony, and handed it invitingly to the chief. The man snarled at him. Lasseter peered around at the deep-lined, savage faces. His eyes alighted on a wizened old man squatting a little apart from the rest. Around his neck hung a small, smoke-blackened fibre bag. Lasseter wished he had offered this man the tea first. He did so now, not with the studied equality of his invitation to the chief, but with deference. The fellow never moved. His little bleared eyes stared straight at Lasseter, who felt those cruel eyes were reading his very thoughts. Lasseter drank the tea himself, smacking his lips with pleasure. The natives hunched eagerly closer in anticipation. He refilled the pannikin and offered it with a "Who's now?" air. An old man slid one leg effortlessly forward, moving his body with it. Lasseter smiled approval.

As this volunteer bent towards him he noticed a huge wart fully six inches long on his back. The old warrior's deeply scarred face had something almost benign in it, which Lasseter sought instantly to cultivate. The native awkwardly tilted the pannikin, got it full of beard, gulped – and choked and coughed with horror and pain.

Despite his anxiety Lasseter had to laugh. He cooled the tea and taught the old man how to drink. Once he got a taste, he clung to the pannikin with both hands till he had noisily drained the last drop. A torrent of guttural inquiries broke out; all wanted to taste, all wanted to smell the tea and watch one another choke. It was an uproarious crowd that pressed around Lasseter while he boiled the billy again and again. Uneasily he saw the water diminishing.

He knew these people would drink it as tea to the last drop if he let them.

He cooked them food and they devoured it ravenously, the hunger sauced by excitement. He showed them rice, and they thought it ants' eggs until they started to eat it raw. It was the most interesting evening of their lives. They talked to him willingly and he understood a lot. But they were constantly suspicious of the food.

"Old Warts", in childlike trust, tasted all food first. Then Lasseter handed the first share to the heathen with the bag; then jovially, a share to the truculent chief who snatched it. Each piccaninny grabbed its share; and lubras shrieked with laughter as at the joke of their lives. Lasseter did all he could to keep up the good impression. He gave them one heavenly meal, right down to the last mouthful. It was all he had. He began to tell them of the white man's food, of its variety and inexhaustible quantity. He built up for them a wealth of food, convoys of it. If they had been a civilized people hearing a plan for making money they could not have listened more greedily.

When Lasseter had talked some of the stars to bed, he stood up and, with a lordly importance, told the crowd that plenty more such food was coming to him – plenty more. To any people who proved his friends he would give plenty such food. Of course, he would have to wait quite a time without food himself, now that his camels had run away. But his white friends were already coming, loading up great foods.

Lasseter well knew these people's lives are one continual struggle for existence. In an often scanty land they must get food or perish. Thus, his offer of an unlimited supply of food represented to them just what unlimited wealth would mean to a civilized man.

Lasseter, father to his wish, and also to work on their superstition, tried to explain how a "great bird" would come from the sky and bring him the foods. But they could not understand. They asked him to draw tracks. Very unwillingly then he described a camel team coming too. With a hoarse bellow the chief was on his feet, his spears clicking, haranguing his tribesmen. He would kill this white dingo before his kamellie drank up all the water! Lasseter loftily waved for silence. He spat in the fire to emphasize his disdain. He explained that the camels would carry most of their own water, in those tin things they had seen on his own camels. And the great bird would carry them the rest.

He won that night. All were for him, the lubras vociferously in his favour. This promise of plentiful, and such wonderful, foods meant life itself to these people, luxurious life. Lasseter allowed them to argue it out, throwing in a word, an expression, an eloquent movement of hands and face, an imaginary patting of a fat stomach to help their imaginations. He put it to these people to supply him with food until his own friends arrived, then he would give them food unlimited. The chief squatted frowning, his eyes to the fire, his corrugated brows voicing his heavy thoughts. The only person who did not speak was the man in the shadows with the bag around his neck.

Lasseter judged the time had come again for him to show independence and unconcern. Yawning ostentatiously, he spread a water sheet, his only covering saved, upon the ground by the fire, and arranged it as if for sleep. Sitting sleepily on the sheet, he pulled out his revolver and toyed with it as if its touch made him oblivious of every presence.

Silently they watched him as he clicked the cylinder, ejected the cartridges, and examined them one by one with a rapt expression on his face. He twirled the cylinder, listening with cocked ear as if its rapid clickings were talking to him, reloaded the weapon, and, with a companionly pat, replaced it in its holster. How he wished he had more than one pocketful of cartridges!

Only when he looked up did he seem to become aware of all those staring eyes. He patted the revolver, hissed "Kaditcha!", stared in the eyes of the chief, and rolled over for sleep.

A deathly silence seized the people; not a whimper broke from the tiniest child. "Kaditcha!" – word of evil!

Lasseter, coiled there with his mind and nerves on edge, felt instinctively all eyes had turned from him to that figure squatting out there in the shadows.

17. THE WITCH-DOCTOR

Next morning the tribe stirred only when the sun grew oppressively hot. Lasseter, sitting up and thinking, dared not disturb them. How far was the nearest water hole, he wondered.

The lubras were the first to stir. The natives slept in rows dug out in the sand, a tiny fire on the ridge between each person. Some slept in a family hole. One by one they sat up, sleepily scowling. A young girl rose, sleepily stretching. She had daubed her breasts and thighs with goanna fat and coloured ochre, and now she was a sand queen.

Pleased interest lighted morose faces as the lubras fanned the fires. They drank the last of the water as tea, and ate the last of the native food. Warts, with a twinkling sort of old smile, explained to Lasseter that the tribe would water and feed him until his own food came. Lasseter heard the verdict with impassive face but thankful heart. He was assured of immediate wants, and could hang out until help arrived.

A stripling came running up, greatly excited. In his hand was a stone splashed with purple-black spots. He had been tracking the camel. Immediately swift runners set out on the camel's track. If the camel was dead or disabled what a gorge of meat the tribe would enjoy. Those that remained eyed Lasseter's revolver, nodding and talking among themselves.

In half an hour the trackers were back, woefully disappointed. The wounded camel's tracks were strong. It was going at a great pace, and would travel many a day yet before it weakened and died. Watta Mitta Mitta, the chief, leaped up, and grasping his spears, strode away. The tribe arose grunting, women snatching pitchis, men their spears. Four young bucks ran out ahead of Watta. The tribe were on the march. Lasseter was pleased. He felt sure the chief would make the pace hot.

Old Warts strode along beside Lasseter, who asked him of the waterhole. The soak Old Warts described was the one Lasseter knew himself, thirty miles away! The country here was mostly long level stretches of sand, growing clumps of desert bush, with ridges of mulga and gidgee trees.

The tribe advanced quickly; the four scouts well ahead, one pair away on the left, the other out on the right. Their distance apart was a shouted "Cooh-hoo!" At centre, but so far behind that he, too was at shouting distance, strode Watta Mitta Mitta, followed by the fighting men. The scouts and the chief thus formed a triangle the base of which would have been a straight line drawn from scouts to scouts. The chief could always see or hear the scouts.

In that manner a tiny party could command a considerable width of country. If the tribe had been going over probable game country, added scouts would have extended the lines miles to right and left. With this formation, game met on centre would find itself within two wide-spread horns, which would close around it as Watta Mitta Mitta's party came up, even though the wind or air-currents blew from the hunters to the hunted.

Lasseter was to admire day by day the thoroughly efficient methods evolved by these stone age men in their ceaseless fight for life.

Mitta Mitta's party consisted of the fighting men and the young bucks soon to be initiated as fighting men. Two hundred yards behind came the old men and boys, not yet striplings, down to lads of five. These, as Lasseter in successive marches quickly observed, were being continuously coached by the old men, instructed exactly as to why such and such a thing was being done by those out in front, told what was likely to happen in such and such an event. The flight of birds overhead was explained; what berries of what trees the birds were making for; what probability of water the flight meant. Especially were the boys taught the meaning of any tracks met; the direction the animal was taking; whether it was fresh or tired, fat or thin, hungry or thirsty, healthy or sick, whether it was seeking a mate. These and many other things the lads learned from the grave-toned old men as they marched. Questions were invited and answered.

Two hundred yards behind this group came the women and toddlers. The women carried the scanty belongings of the tribe and the babes too young to walk. These were carried sometimes on the hip, sometimes across the small of the back, the mother's arms crooked around the neck and heels of the child, thus leaving her hands free while the child suckled the breast.

Occasionally a man would fall back from the main body and carry his babe over a bad patch of country should the mother be sick. The men carried only their spears and wommeras – the throwing stick. That was not altogether due to laziness. The law of the survival of the quick and the ready demanded that the able-bodied men should be ready on the instant to hunt or to fight.

This first day, Lasseter had cause to admire the walking powers of these people. Without apparent effort long graceful strides were taking them easily over the country at a surprising rate. When the tribe was sure that all was clear ahead, some of the men dropped back from Mitta Mitta's party while smaller children came up from the women. These youngsters stepped in the footsteps of their fathers, solemn-faced kids, staring at the ground, grasping toy spears, intensely preoccupied with the business of life. Lasseter, always interested in and fond of children, even these desert products, noticed that the fathers shortened their stride for the younger children while imperceptibly increasing the pace. A child ten years old could stride in the unfettered steps of his father.

Hour after hour that tireless walk kept on. Lasseter thanked his lucky stars that he was in fair condition. Soon he was thirsty, but he dared not show any sign of distress. How he envied the power in the bony, thin legs of these people, all sinew and muscle! Later he began to envy the children their walking powers.

Old Warts took from behind his ear a half-chewed plug of pituri, made from the pituri shrub. It was greasy-looking stuff, like a hard roll of coarse tobacco. Lasseter bit off a chew. When he became properly "native" he appreciated this apparent narcotic that, chewed in moderation, helped against fatigue.

Before sundown they arrived at the soak. Lasseter threw himself down and drank like an animal as the others did. He lay there in deep thankfulness. He had survived the first day; had paced it out with the tribe. Would he be able to last out tomorrow? As the blacks squatted and talked round their little fires, he listened for news of water and food. There was no food. This was merely a rock-hole which caught water from other rocks when it rained. In this particular locality there was no game, nor were there any edible roots.

Old Warts explained, as he dug a great thorn from his toes, that tomorrow at sundown they would eat. In the valley of the waterhole there were yams; they would get there early and the women would dig. Warts said it was only a little way – "one sit down". Lasseter was miserably intrigued. He knew that, in the dry season, when numbers of the soaks dry up, these people were capable of walking a hundred miles between drinks.

However, it was not as bad as that. This "sit down" meant only twenty miles. Lying stretched flat out staring at the stars, Lasseter became conscious of the "Kaditcha silence". Impossible to describe that eerie condition – like a civilized man sensing the presence of a ghost!

Lasseter stared at the wizened figure squatting in the shadow. He had taken the bag from round his neck and was now, with an indefinable air of mystery, placing the contents on the ground before his crossed shanks. With skinny claw the witch-doctor pulled out a dried lizard, laid it down and stared at it for minutes. Then his lips moved sibilantly and Lasseter could have sworn that the lizard hissed in reply. Quick as thought

Lasseter nodded as if in understanding. Then appeared, in succession, a string of dried berries, an eagle's claw, some water-worn pebbles of queer shapes and colours, a quartz crystal, and a handful of yellowed human knuckle-bones. Over each article he pored as if actually conversing with it, as if it possessed some power of evil. And to each exhibit Lasseter gave recognition; his solemn noddings confirming that which was suggested by their owner. He never once glanced at the staring eyes around; he felt their terror. Only the older men dared stare at the witch-doctor. The children had long since buried their faces deep in their mothers' breasts. The women sat with their backs turned, their eyes fast closed as they crouched over the children.

The sorcerer next took from the bag a little red ball. He stared at this a long time, then began unwinding wrappings of red fibre so fine it might have been red cloth. Lasseter wondered what desert plant had supplied that fibre. He thought of the mummies of Egypt. The last wrappings revealed a tiny skull, polished ivory white. That skull was so small that the baby it once was could hardly have been born. Then came the culminating symbol of his power. With a snakelike movement the man's arm withdrew a thin package about ten inches long wrapped in tea-tree bark as thin as brown paper. Coiled round the bundle was a plaited cord of human hair. Then, for the first time, the eyes of the witch-doctor glared evilly towards Lasseter. He knew!

The small package carried the death bone!

Lasseter, with a knowing inclination of the head and an expressive stare, acknowledged this emblem of life and death. In sepulchral tones Lasseter turned to Old Warts and congratulated him and the tribe on their witch-doctor, who held greater Kaditcha than any other black doctor. It was only because he knew each of these Kaditchas so perfectly himself, and could control them, that he understood how powerful this witch-doctor really was.

Then Lasseter rolled himself in his ground sheet as if for sleep. But he was listening, though exultation ran through his veins. He could feel that he had pulled through again. The witch-doctor's display had been a challenge directed against his revolver Kaditcha of the night before. He had turned this challenge to his advantage. He had confirmed the tribe in their belief that the witch-doctor was the genuine article, and so had pleased him mightily. Lasseter felt sure of that. At the same time he had impressed the tribe with his own power, and thereby made them yet more in awe of that mysterious little Kaditcha he carried in his belt.

18. THE LOST 'PLANE

Taylor hurried his camels on the three-hundred-mile trip to Ilbilba only to find that he had to wait for the 'plane. A long wait it proved.

His first care on arrival was to examine the supply dump. Nothing was touched. He unlashed the tarpaulin, thrust his hand underneath, and nearly fell over himself at a warning hiss. Gingerly hauling off the tarpaulin, he blinked at a fat carpet snake. It rose upon its coils, shot out its tongue, and hissed vindictively. In the subsequent brawl the reptile fought determinedly for its right of possession.

Some of Taylor's old native acquaintances were camped by the soak. He bargained with them to scout out and watch from the hills for the 'plane, and to "smoke-talk" to distant myalls for signs of the great bird. An old buck, much excited, came running to him with news of a big savage tribe "two sit downs" away, engaged in initiation rites. Taylor asked him to tell them to come in. He would hire them as watchers upon the hills. The old chap scratched his beard doubtfully, but at the price of a tin of meat set out with his wives to "smoke-talk".

Next day he returned with the answer that the tribe was too busy "making young men". After the ceremonies were finished they might pay the white fellow a visit if they were "not tired".

The big bird did not come. Taylor was jumpy. Was this desert hoodoo still flying with the Company's 'planes?

Christmas Day was more reliable than the 'plane. Taylor was unaware he was not the only one waiting on that Christmas Day. A little girl in Gippsland was waiting; a girl in Wagga too. And Lasseter's wife in Sydney had been promised he would be home by Christmas. Taylor knew Lasseter must be waiting somewhere and – Where the hell were Hamre and Pittendrigh?

From Alice Springs to Ilbilba was a flight of only four hours and the *Golden Quest II* had been scheduled to leave on the 20th!

Taylor must do something, so he prepared his Christmas pudding. The dough was so sticky that when he brushed the flies away some of them stuck to his fingers. They looked like currants when in the dough. It was a relief when he thought of the old folks in England. Was it snowing with them? The cottage roof must be all white. There would be mistletoe under the kitchen porch. Dreamily he stared out across the desert fringe.

While the pudding was cooking he would make his "parade". He strolled all over the landing-ground, making sure no ant-hills had sprung up in the night. The ants there build at overtime rate and a new ant-hill where it should not be on a 'drome is liable to wreck a 'plane on landing. He inspected the piled heaps of brushwood that were in readiness for his signal flares. The beacons were crying for the match. He felt inclined to light one, the dry pile was so tempting. He felt like a boy who wanted to let off crackers.

It was dinner-time now, so he sat down to his pudding – and found it a Christmas sod. He had put stuff in it that wouldn't rise. Ah, well, no matter! His mind was too busy listening for the drone of a 'plane to detect the difference between salt and baking-soda.

In the afternoon he read and re-read old letters, wondering what his old people were doing; if his "Big Stick" was safely housed; if Pittendrigh carried a home mail for him in the 'plane.

Natives came running to Taylor. The "big bird" had been seen days before flying away to the north.

"Saddle up the fastest camel," said Taylor to Johns. "Ride day and night to Hermannsburg Mission. Ask the Superintendent to wireless Alice Springs and the directors. Get away now, and keep going!"

In twenty minutes Johns had set out on his lonely two-hundred-mile ride. His camel was fresh; he rode day and night.

The Mission broadcast the news. In minutes, almost, people all over the continent were listening in to the report that two men were missing somewhere out in the great heart of Australia. A camel search-party was organized at the mission; natives were hurried out far and wide to "smoke-talk" to "friendly" wild tribes. The Government Resident at Alice Springs sent out camel parties; the Police organized parties. It was a race against time.

The directors asked the Defence Department to aid in the search. Two R.A.A.F. 'planes under Flight-Lieutenant Eaton and Flying-Officer Gerrand, left Point Cook at daylight *en route* for the Centre. Their Moth 'planes were specially equipped, extra fuelling tanks giving them a thousand miles cruising range. Eaton was not new to a job like this. He was in charge of the Air Force party which participated in the search for Keith Anderson and Hitchcock after their tragic Centralian flight in 1929.

The Defence 'planes reached Alice Springs, arranged with the Government Resident to send out ground parties to cooperate in the air search, then flew to Hermannsburg and on to Ilbilba. No trace of the missing 'plane was seen.

Taylor and his native scouts heard a 'plane afar off. Taylor ran to the signal beacons, apprehensively gazing up at the 'plane he knew was not the *Golden Quest*.

"They've failed to locate Ilbilba and run out of petrol," he said to Eaton. "They've come down somewhere between here and Alice Springs. I've got all the natives I can muster 'smoke-talking' across the desert, but you are the first definite news I've had."

Desperate efforts were made to find the missing men. It was known they had set out on their flight with only thirty-nine gallons of petrol, six gallons of water, and a week's food supply. The search continued for a fortnight with no trace. Hamre's wife in Sydney became desperately anxious. Two more R.A.A.F. 'planes, under Flying-Officer A. N. Evans and Flying-Officer B. E. M. Dalton, hurried to the search – all looking for a little 'plane whose black wings would be so hard to see amongst the mulga.

Camel parties were scouring two thousand miles of country. Hope was waning. Only one man in all Alice Springs believed the men would be found alive. So strong was his faith that he bet a case of bottled beer on it!

Taylor, anxious to send out every native he could in a search from the Ilbilba end, remembered that tribe so busy "making men". They were now completing their ceremonies on "sacred" ground, only half a day away. He secured a guide and hurried across to buy their aid. For natives to dance and sing while white men were perishing was ridiculous!

They heard a wild chant through the trees, accompanied by a thrumming and a stamping in savagely rising cadences that set their hearts beating faster. Wisps of smoke filtered through the tree branches. Presently they came on a wild scene, hemmed in by rocks. A crowd of naked men and women had been worked up to an hysterical pitch by superstition. Smoke from tiny fires drifted among bodies glistening in sweat and animal oil. Their bodies were striped with bands of crimson, yellow, and white ochre. Stiff stalks of coloured grass were thrust through their noses; their greased hair was banded back from corrugated foreheads with plaitings of animal hide and grass. The old men were the masters of ceremonies, the old lubras their shrieking assistants. Like black witches they gloated in the frenzy of the crowd and the pain of the victims. Painted warriors stood a little aside, glaring at the scene, their hands convulsively clenching, their feet uncontrollably stamping. Young lubras pushed among the groups, taunting the young men, daring them to cry out. Not the slightest notice was taken of the white man. A stripling was grasped by the arms and without protest thrust in amongst a group and stood upon a heap of dry kindling. A withered lubra, kneeling by his feet, held up dry tinder and shrieked to him how it would crackle, and blaze up, and burn, burn, burn! Another old lubra clawed over his body, spitting upon him, her toothless gums frothing. A lubra applied a firestick and the tinder blazed up, its brisk crackling accompanied by a howling chant. The lubras danced in mad abandon, shrieking to the boy to cry out. As he was enveloped by smoke his eyes began to bulge, his body trembled, and the muscles twitched in glistening relief. From his tight-shut lips came never a moan. A heavy white smoke enveloped that group, from which came cries and glimpses of writhing limbs like a picture of fiends in hell.

They were burning the boy's feet, they were trying to make him cry out – if they could. Had he called out, had he even moaned, he would have failed in this, his initiation into warriorhood. He would be scoffed at by the young women; he would not be allowed a wife; he would have to suffer the same ceremony in another twelve moons. "I would not be a wild nigger," thought Taylor, as he walked back to camp, "for all the tea in China!"

19. THE FORCED LANDING

The 20th of December was a warm, bright day when the *Golden Quest II* roared skyward from Alice Springs aerodrome. Both men were eager to get in touch with the gold-seekers. Hamre's ears, muffled by the cap-flaps and ear-phones, soon got used to the noise. He leaned his face over the fuselage, seeking a cool breeze, but the air rushing past was hot and parched. He gazed down on a range of mountains, attracted by the peculiar peaks like jagged spires. But the 'plane travelled so fast that soon he was gazing on a sea of mulga tops with occasional hills breaking the surface, like islands miles apart. The ever-receding horizon was a semi-circle of mountains and grey plain.

The *Golden Quest II* throbbed like a thing of life, soaring gloriously over those sombre lands below. Hamre felt confidently aloof, thrilled at the mastery of man over earth. But he shuddered at the thought of what a forced landing down there might mean. He heard the booming voice of Pittendrigh through the ear-phones:

"These damn maps are all to blazes! They show identical hills fifty miles apart."

"That looks like our spot," bawled Hamre through his mouthpiece, "that plain down there between the two ranges. Ilbilba ought to be just by the foothills of the Ehrenbergs."

"Yes!" bellowed the answer. "And that range over there looks like this range over here; and this plain down here looks like that plain twenty miles back!"

"I don't see any smoke signals yet," said Hamre, hopefully.

"Of course you don't," bellowed Pittendrigh, "because they're not lit yet. If there are any eagle eyes down below I wish they'd wave a firestick."

Rather anxiously Hamre gazed, wondering how the petrol was holding out. They only had five and a half hours' supply aboard. The engine was going beautifully; but time was speeding too. Time flies when in the air. "That stupid-looking pimple down there looks like what Mount Russell should look like," bawled Pittendrigh, as he swooped low in a long circle preparatory to turning back. Presently his voice came to Hamre:

"Fifteen minutes' petrol left. Am looking for a landing."

Hamre's heart leapt. A forced landing here! Then he strained his eyes at the immediate danger, seeking a landing-ground in this sea of timber.

"Where are you going to land?" he yelled.

"On the ground!" bawled Pittendrigh. "That should be Haast's Bluff."

The engine spluttered violently and Hamre's heart raced. A threatening "Honk! Honk!" made him grasp the cockpit. He shouted to Pittendrigh, who nodded in reply as below them opened out a tiny patch of waving wheat. Pittendrigh immediately swooped towards the grass patch, a veritable oasis to the failing machine. Pittendrigh swooped low, manoeuvring to land against the wind. That was impossible, so he chanced it skilfully and the big bird settled above the grass. Hamre clutched the cockpit, anticipating vine-hidden logs and stumps; but the 'plane landed quite gently and ran along the ground to the threshing of grass.

Pittendrigh climbed from the cockpit, remarking, "That's that!" as he scratched his ear.

"That is that!" answered Hamre, as he climbed thankfully from the machine. Pittendrigh, his big form erect above the grass, stood gazing around with the interest of a schoolboy. They stood on a narrow grass flat, walled in by drab mulga, around them a great silence, a heat that burned, a faint hum of insects!

"Well, let us eat!" declared Pittendrigh jovially.

In a thoughtful silence Hamre lit a fire and put the billy on. The crackling twigs were tinder to his thoughts.

"Hell, it is hot!" he exclaimed, stepping back.

"Sure it is!" assured Pittendrigh agreeably. "The parsons say so, and we can't contradict until we arrive there. But anyway, now we'll have Christmas in Alice Springs for sure. Roast duck and turkey. What-ho! Where's the jolly old tea?"

Again Hamre looked at this big Englishman, war ace and flying man around Australian cities. Then he gazed up at the brazen sky. Surely Pittendrigh did not realize the peril they were in, the menace of distances, of thirst. Quietly he made the tea. Pittendrigh was already carrying the food to the nearest shade.

That was the last tea they drank for exactly three weeks.

Lolling there in the shade, they rolled cigarettes and discussed a course of action. Finally they decided to attempt the walk back to Alice Springs. "We might strike a river," explained Pittendrigh brightly, and added, "Why look so solemn? Anything might happen in this country."

"Yes!" grunted Hamre, "it might!"

They put the seat, engine, and prop covers on the machine, then tied it down.

"Snug as a bug in a rug," declared Pittendrigh admiringly, as he wiped his brow. "Oh, for a pint of bitter!"

"Dry up," growled Hamre.

In Pittendrigh's mosquito net they wrapped five tins of mixed meats, half a bottle of malted milk tabloids, and two small packets each containing six thick biscuits. They filled three water-bags with about four gallons of water, and carried the machine's compass in the billycan. Hamre looked longingly at the revolver in the 'plane before they set out. They had been unable to procure cartridges to fit it in Alice Springs.

Immediately they entered the mulga they were hemmed in; short-growing, almost shadeless timber closed around them. Soon they were bathed in sweat, and presently were pestered with an itching at the legs from the needle points of countless grass-seeds. As they pushed through the grass their trousers became black with the pests boring right into the skin.

"These dashed seeds grow points like needles," growled Pittendrigh, as he vainly brushed his trouser legs. "And those curly little tails of theirs – what are they for!"

"So that the point will bore in like an auger," explained Hamre, "and get a firm grip on anything that brushes through the grass. Animals carry these seeds a long way. It's one of Nature's little ideas for scattering her seed far and wide."

"That's all very well," growled Pittendrigh, "but I'm not a dashed incubator for grass-seeds!"

Hamre was suffering from a nasty war-wound in the leg, which did not help in such rough walking. Dog-tired from pushing through the scrub, they halted at sundown.

"Can't see where we've jolly well come from," said Pittendrigh, as he gazed back into the mulga. "All we've got to show for our walk is sweat and grass-seeds."

Of their three boxes of wax vestas, two were completely ruined, the heads soft from sweat. With almost frantic fear Hamre opened the third box. The heads were dry! Night settled down stuffy and hot. They drew well away from the big fires they had lit in the hope of attracting natives. They were very thirsty. Pittendrigh woefully examined the tobacco supply – one pouch full. The tobacco had absorbed so much sweat that it wouldn't light. A firestick held hard to a cigarette end only made it smell – horribly.

Pittendrigh sprawled out with a sigh. Hamre stared into the night watching the sky for any reflection of answering fires. As they talked he listened.

"Cheerful land," mused Pittendrigh, as with head pillowed upon his hands he gazed up at the stars. "Flowing with mulga and sand and white ants! I wonder what they're doing at the Ambassadors tonight?"

"Dash the Ambassadors! We've got to think of the course to the Alice, of time and waterholes."

"Why not think of the Ambassadors?" argued Pittendrigh, mildly. "We've got just as much hope of dining there."

Hamre glanced at him, then listened, hoping against hope for the shouted call of a native. Not even the howl of a dingo broke the stillness.

They pushed on at daylight and the heat gradually enveloped them.

"Isn't it awful!" grunted Hamre, as his legs twisted under him and he sat on a dead branch hidden under the grass.

"The cheeks of my body are running a banker with sweat!" groaned Pittendrigh.

By midday their water was running short. Pittendrigh's light shoes were coming apart. Hamre threw away his leggings as so much useless weight. Tired by the heat and constant pushing through bushes, they halted, seeking shade, and, opening a tin of sausages, tasted hungrily. Mutely they gazed at one another, then threw the tin away.

The sausages were salty!

"See those little hills over there?" pointed Hamre. "We'll reach them tonight and light beacon fires. Some natives may see them. Come on."

But if any native saw the fires that night he made never a sign. They trod doggedly on next day well into the afternoon.

"Veer over to the south, Pitt," suggested Hamre, a bit throatily. "Make for the line of ranges. We may find water in some gully."

They reached the foothills before sundown and crossed a number of gullies, all as dry as a bone.

"Like me," said Pittendrigh. "When I get back I'll buy a pub!" At sundown they climbed a hill.

"All one damn hill after another," growled Pittendrigh as they gazed on hills rising into crags already enveloped by the purple shadows of evening.

"It's rather lonesome," said Hamre.

"So much so," answered Pittendrigh definitely, "that a morgue would be rowdy in comparison!"

Right on top of the hill stood a dead tree. They dragged bushes around it and set it alight, eating their evening tabloid to a display of fireworks. The tree blazed royally, a torch that should have been visible many miles away.

"The jolly old niggers will see that and come running from all their cubby holes," declared Pittendrigh enthusiastically. "And if only they skin their feet like I've skinned mine I'll be satisfied!"

Hamre smiled. "Where does the map say we are?" he inquired.

"Any old where at all," declared Pittendrigh. "One map says we're in Central Australia, and the other swears we're in the West. Have your choice."

Hamre stared glumly at the blazing tree.

"Like a jolly old Father Christmas," said Pittendrigh, as he moved away from the blazing sparks. "There are thousands of cold children in England would love this."

At daylight the tree still stood, but now it was a pole of charcoal. The men left their few tinned meats, fearing the treacherous saltiness, and trudged on into another blazing day.

20. THE LONG, LONG TREK

It was midday when Hamre gasped: "Pitt, if we don't drink the last of the water the sun will. It's nearly all evaporated."

"Let us cool our little insides then," replied Pittendrigh, thickly. "The sun can go to blazes!"

Their eyes were bloodshot, their lips parched as each drank with delicious relief. The fluff from the bags tickled their throats as they sucked in the last draughts of cool air.

"Nectar from the gods!" sighed Pittendrigh. "I can feel it oozing right to the roots of my hair."

Hamre looked towards the brazen sun which had stolen the water even as they walked. He gazed away out over at a far-flung horizon of grey mulga tops; shading his eyes at the empty sky, he searched around the sombre mountains. Not the faintest wisp of smoke. Not the slightest indication of water to any man who did not know where the hidden soaks lay.

"Fine panorama, isn't it?" volunteered Pittendrigh affably. "And you can see it all for nothing!"

"Pitt," said Hamre seriously, "we both know how things are. Have you any suggestion to make, any scheme at all to pull through?"

"None whatever, old bean," admitted Pittendrigh cheerfully, "except one."

"What is that?" demanded Hamre hopefully.

"Let us die like gentlemen, in comfort." And Pittendrigh knelt clumsily to fix his ragged mosquito-net in the shade of a mulga tree.

Hamre grunted hoarsely as he staggered away to crawl under the shade of a thin-branched tree. Stripped to the waist, he lay face to the ground, seeking cool air at the roots of the tree.

Around them settled a stifling silence. Time passed. Hamre heard – he thought he was dreaming for the sound was so minute, yet sharply clear and distinct – an energetic scratching, a boring as a wee insect worked his home into hard dry wood. Hours passed. From a great distance there came a faint humming, rapidly growing into a thunderous buzz. It was coming through the sky directly towards them, dodging the mulga trees. Hamre's subconscious mind struggled with his body against the conflicting urge to jump erect, yet be quite still. His mind won as the blowfly buzzed harshly around him.

"I hope it will wait a little while," he thought, with thoughts that were far away. His tongue was swelling now: he could feel it growing in his mouth like a big overnight potato. He wondered if it kept on swelling would he choke. This was the beginning of the end, he knew, for Hamre had been years in the Western Australian bush.

A snowflake touched his bare burnt back, a fairy touch, like a kiss from a maiden's lips. Body and mind tingled on the instant, his heart pounded like the roar of a flying engine. He leapt straight up through the bushes, staring at a rolling black cloud overhead from which spat down a grey sheet.

"Pitt! Pitt!" he cried. "Rain! Rain! Rain!"

In all that vast land, one small rain-cloud had settled directly above the men, and burst.

They threw off their rags; open-mouthed they waved their arms and jumped up at the cloud, and laughed, and yelled. Had natives witnessed this madness they would have declared them to be of the Kaditcha.

Hamre spread his singlet and Pittendrigh stretched out the sleeves, laughing as the fat raindrops splashed mud from it. In half a minute the singlet was "running". They wrung it into the billycan and gulped the water.

"Tastes good to me," gurgled Pittendrigh. "I've heard about the jolly old boys bathing Cleopatra in champagne and quaffing the bathwater. But any port in a storm does me!"

"It's a miracle," said Hamre, fervently. "I will never growl at rain again, no matter how hard it rains as long as I live!"

"Neither will I," agreed Pittendrigh devoutly, "and I'll never swear again either!" But he did.

Rooting energetically, they scratched a hole in the sand and directed rivulets into it, laughing as they plastered one another with mud. They quickly filled the bags with the muddy water.

Hamre stood erect, serious in his reaction. The rain was purely a local shower. Even as he thought, the last drops ceased. This miracle from a blazing sky put new heart into them; filled them with the desire to live.

"We're not supposed to die of thirst anyway," declared Pittendrigh. "This reminds me of the man they couldn't hang!"

"They must have stretched his neck though," said Hamre, as he drank again.

"Yes," gulped Pittendrigh, "that's what I did to mine when I was reaching for those raindrops."

It was late, but they started walking again, cheerful in the smell of the moist bush, finding the way not so hard, the going not so rough.

"As full of hope," Pittendrigh declared, "as a butcher's pup is of meat!"

That evening a broad line of trees barred their way.

"A creek," exclaimed Hamre as he pushed on with revived hope, "and a big one."

"There'll be water in it, sure as the gods made little apples!" declared Pittendrigh.

There was. They walked right onto a decent pool. Hamre smiled as he knelt down gratefully to drink as much as he liked. This pool meant yet another reprieve.

Next morning a chill dawn soon warmed into a hot day. Steam rose from the ground and before eleven o'clock there was nothing to tell that rain had fallen only the afternoon before. The grass-seeds, sharp and stiff again, pierced through their clothes with revitalized energy. The heat from the sand scorched their faces as the day wore slowly on. Their legs were dragging when suddenly they came across a rough bough shelter.

"It's not recent," said Hamre in answer to their sudden hope. "It was built by the niggers months ago."

"It'll do me," sighed Pittendrigh. "What's good enough for a nigger is not to be sneezed at in this land!"

He crawled under the boughs and stretched out in the cool shade. Hamre threw off all his clothes and did likewise. The coolness bathed their aching bodies. They stared through the black rotting branches at the blaze of sunlight outside. The recent presence of animals came pungently to their nostrils. They did not care.

"It's not eau de cologne," said Pittendrigh sleepily, "and it's not lavender. But what would you expect in a boudoir like this!"

Presently Hamre began scratching. Lying on his side, too tired to roll over, he just scratched. He scratched again, sighing plaintively at the tiring necessity. Then scratched again and again, and –

"What the heliotrope blazes are you scratching at?" demanded Pittendrigh. "I can't get a wink. If we are slipping back to the stone age, don't degenerate into the monkey so quickly. Enjoy a civilized scratch and be done with it!"

But Hamre scratched and scratched. He sat up. Pittendrigh stared at the mottled black marks all down the side of Hamre's body.

"What on earth is it?" he asked aghast.

"Hanged if I know. I wish you had taken your clothes off too, instead of being so lazy. You're the fattest!"

"I'm a feather-bed cave-man," grinned Pittendrigh. "My lily-white skin is a beauty parlour beside yours. By Jove," he added fervently, "what a hide Adam must have had. No wonder Eve wore a fig leaf!"

Hamre broke off a sharp-pointed twig, dug into the hard ground, and unearthed what looked like a black coffee-bean, cut lengthways.

"What on earth is it?" asked Pittendrigh.

Hamre stuck the twig into it, and the thing squirted blood. "Kangaroo bugs!" said Hamre decisively.

"Lor' luv us," breathed Pittendrigh. "Who wouldn't be a kangaroo? No wonder they hop!"

Hamre crawled out of the shelter and struck a match.

"What are you going to do?"

"Burn it."

"Hold hard! They haven't bitten me – yet!"

"Well stay there until they do."

Pittendrigh didn't. He hurriedly left when the branches began to crackle. The men stepped back as the tinder-dry mass shot up in flame.

They tramped on again, blessing any rise in the country from which they might spy clearer ground.

"That might be Mount Hay," pointed Pittendrigh, doubtfully. The mount showed hazily distant over the treetops.

"It might, again it mightn't!" answered Hamre.

"Let's make hay while the sun shines," suggested Pittendrigh, hopefully. "There might be something to eat over there!"

"Yes," answered Hamre, "carrots!"

At sundown two very weary men camped. Hamre was the bushman. He lit the fire, jealous of their one box of matches. Pittendrigh had attempted a fire once, and his cheerful lighting of match after match had filled Hamre with horror. They ate a milk tabloid each, then frugally rolled a cigarette. At an allowance of two smokes each a day they calculated their tobacco would last another five days.

"Glorious weed!" sighed Pittendrigh, as he smoked until the cigarette-stump burnt his lips. "That mildew in the tobacco doesn't seem to harm it either. A peculiar sweat you must exude."

"You drank the water from the singlet and didn't seem to notice it," retaliated Hamre.

"Yes, by Jove!" soliloquized Pittendrigh. "I wonder if it has grown any fungus in our little Mary's. Perhaps that's what we're living on!"

Hamre smiled. "Isn't it awful!" he sighed.

Pittendrigh burst out laughing. "Now, now," he admonished.

Hamre had slipped again. "Isn't it awful!" was a lifelong expression of his. He had promised not to use it so often under these circumstances. Just as Pittendrigh had promised not to swear. Hamre really did try to check any thoughtless words that might have an adverse moral effect on their chances.

"Never fear," reassured Pittendrigh, "the big birds will surely find us."

But Hamre gazed out on the darkening night and could see little chance of rescue. Pittendrigh had an abiding faith in aeroplanes. Hamre's faith went more to a ground-party sooner or later cutting their tracks.

From the aeroplane to their present position was a seventy-mile line now. If any search party travelled between them and the 'plane they must pick up their tracks. No land party would find them in time if their tracks or a smoke signal were not sighted. They needed their big fire that night; a drizzle fell, blotting out the stars. They shivered all night.

"Why the purple blazes they can't build mosquito nets to keep out rain as well as skeeters, I don't know," growled Pittendrigh.

In a cold misty morning they came to the conclusion that they were both getting beaten: they felt their weakness very definitely. They were desperately hungry; and the only sure water they knew of was back at the big creek. They decided to return and wait there for the end, one way or the other. By resting near water their strength would last much longer. If they pushed on and found no water, then endurance would be only a matter of hours. They turned back. It was a hard day.

"The best of friends must part," sighed Pittendrigh ruefully, as he left the last of his socks on a bush.

It was a rather miserable night, sitting there by the fire, Pittendrigh nursing the blisters on his heels, Hamre picking grass-seeds out of his legs.

21. CHRISTMAS ON THE DESERT FRINGE

"Christmas day in the workhouse," growled Pittendrigh as they trudged wearily back. "And my shoes are wearing out. Now I can appreciate the dire straits of your Australian poet when his pants began to go. Fancy sitting down on these twigs with nothing on behind!"

But Hamre was silent, trying to devise some means of helping those who might be searching for them. The world seemed very big and bright out here. That they should be forced to lie down and die in the prime of their strength seemed a dreadful thing – a wasteful thing.

In celebration of Christmas, they ate one milk tabloid each.

"Roast beef and turkey," groaned Pittendrigh, as he sat tenderly on a soft patch of sand, "is being devoured by millions today. We, however, have achieved a record in these days of records. I'll wager we are the only two men in the world who are dining this Christmas on a milk tabloid!" And he critically surveyed the meal lying like a white pill on his big palm.

"Eat and be merry!" grinned Hamre.

"Amen!" grunted Pittendrigh, as he swallowed his pill. Their first thought when back at the big creek was the waterhole. To their intense relief it was still there, though already showing distinct signs of evaporation. They set about building a bough shelter against their enemy the sun; the job was almost completed by evening. An aboriginal might have waxed sarcastic over the gunyah, but not so Pittendrigh. Solemnly he raised his arms aloft in blessing.

"Noble building, babe of the sweat of our brow, I name thee 'Hamreville'." He waited for the approbation which did not come, then exclaimed, "I say, old son, I'm jolly hungry!"

"Really?"

"Decidedly so!"

"Of course I'm not?"

"Then why don't we go back for the meat!"

Hamre stared. The tinned meats of course. The next morning early they set out on a most cheerful walk, for was not there a meal at the end of it?

"A-shopping we will go," bawled Pittendrigh. Then he swore violently as he barked his shin on a fallen log. Hamre marvelled at the joviality of the man.

Arrived back in the locality, they searched until they could hardly drag one foot after the other.

"It's no good, Ham old boy, we're euchred! It's like looking for a needle in a haystack."

"No, no; keep on," urged Hamre. "We can last another hour. Look for the big burned tree; it must still be standing."

Happy thought! But the hour was quite gone when they located the burned tree afar off. The tins were where they had left them. They swung their hats in the air and gave three cheers for the burned tree; then opened a tin and ate ravenously. Too full for words, but not full enough for comfort, they lay there gazing longingly at the three tins of meat that were left. Sixteen malted milk tablets were counted three times over to make sure none had been missed.

Next morning they started back to Hamreville. Twenty minutes later Pittendrigh grumbled: "Surprising how heavy this damn water-bag gets. It is gaining weight instead of losing."

"It won't be heavy when we get to the creek," answered Hamre. It wasn't: it was empty.

"Here commenceth the siege," said Pittendrigh as he crawled into the gunyah.

As they lay there, two small lizards emerged from the branches and scurried upside down along the ridge-pole, seeking flies. The men stared up – two minds with but a single thought.

"Too thin," voiced Pittendrigh disappointedly. Hamre sighed.

"I wonder if they'll grow?" went on Pittendrigh. "They're lively little beggars: they can run along that ridge-pole a dashed sight faster than I can use my feet. Sh, he's got a fly!"

Hungrily the men watched.

"Good job there are plenty of flies," said Pittendrigh. "I never appreciated them before. I wonder if they are fattening?"

"Don't talk so loud," admonished Hamre. "You might scare them."

"There," exclaimed Pittendrigh, "the other lizard's nailed one. Watch him scoff it. Bully boy!"

Hamre stared up, calculating the length of the lizards. They seemed young ones. Perhaps, in time –

"Call 'em Tom and Joe," said Pittendrigh. "I'll bet you a dollar Tom gets fattest first!"

"Done!" agreed Hamre.

And they shook hands on it. Waiting his chance, Pittendrigh caught a fly upon his neck, impaled it on a straw, and invitingly held it up to "Tom".

Tom arched down his neck, his beady little eyes twinkling; there flashed a tiny long tongue and the fly was gone. Pittendrigh drew a deep breath of satisfaction.

"I'll have you so your hams will stand out like horses' shanks!" he declared.

Hamre immediately set about catching a fly for "Joe".

At dawn both men awoke to a shrieking, guttural chorus that rang among the trees. Hastily they crawled out, and were greeted by an outburst of raucous shrieks. The trees on the creek-bank were covered with black cockatoos. Hamre's eyes glistened.

"Oh, for a gun!" breathed Pittendrigh.

Stealthily they crawled from the gunyah. They need not have been so cautious. The big birds greeted them with coarse remarks, as if aware of their helplessness. The men collected an armful of stones and sneaked under a tree. At the first ineffectual volley the cockatoos flapped heavily to another tree, shrieking hoarsely.

"That's that!" said Pittendrigh.

"It is that!" answered Hamre.

Two more milk tabloids were eaten that day and the remaining fourteen, with the three tins of meat, counted again. Towards evening the cockatoos flew noisily away.

The following day was stiflingly hot. Flies swarmed into the gunyah and ants came with them. The cockatoos were back again, their raucous calls ringing through the trees. Hamre sat in the gunyah trying to make a shanghai out of the elastic of his motor goggles. He was bitterly disappointed when he found the elastic too weak to throw a stone any distance. The birds seemed to jeer at him. Pittendrigh strolled along the creek. He returned with his hands full of weeds.

"Looks like mint," he said hopefully.

"Looks like grass," replied Hamre.

"I'm going to boil it, anyway. It might taste like mint."

"Might taste like buttercups!"

Pittendrigh boiled it; both men ate it. The stuff tasted like nothing on earth.

"Things are not what they seem," sighed Pittendrigh. "Let us devour a tabloid instead."

That night was bitterly cold. The men longed for blankets as they shivered by the fire, roasting one side of their bodies then the other. They swore at the cockatoos when a black cloud of them came swishing over at daylight. Another cloud came, too – a pink cloud, beautiful under the sun, a cloud of galahs. The men gazed longingly at the plump birds.

"All that meat going to waste," sighed Pittendrigh; "they'll die some day and blow away in dust."

Another cloud flashed towards them, a shimmering green cloud that almost hid the sun. The cloud split in twain and the sun shone through. Then the halves flashed together and the united cloud sped up and down in glorious undulations; then split again, reunited, wheeled, and in an instant the trees were robed with green parakeets.

"Beautiful!" said Hamre. "But I wish we were bird catchers."

"If we could only put salt on their tails!" sighed Pittendrigh. He walked slowly towards the creek, but had hardly gone fifty yards when he stood, staring at the imprint of a camel's pad on the sand. Excitedly the men examined the track.

"He crossed the creek when we went back to look for the tinned stuff," said Hamre, dismayed. "Isn't it awful!"

Pittendrigh laughed accusingly.

They collected stones to throw at birds. Neither man spoke of the shock of discovering how weak he was. In the gunyah they lay staring up at the ridge-pole.

"Tom is growing just a little fatter, don't you think?" asked Pittendrigh, critically.

"If he doesn't improve more rapidly than that he'll dine on us and not we on him," mumbled Hamre.

Pittendrigh, scratching around for his notebook, sat up and said, "Let's have a game of cricket."

Hamre looked at him, wondering.

"It's all right," reassured Pittendrigh. "I'm not off my pitch yet. We'll really have a game of cricket and you'll find it very interesting. See, I divide the paper like this and put these letters and numbers in the squares:

7	5	B	1	5
	9	6	D	4
10	L.B.W.	3	5	0
3	C	16	S	

"The numbers represent the number of runs made at each bat. The letter D stands for duck; L.B.W. for leg before wicket; C for caught; and so on. We toss up. I'll do it with a legitimate shilling – I've only got one or two by the way. What is it?"

"Heads," answered Hamre, disinterestedly.

"Ah, heads it is! Now, you go in first while I keep the score. You take the book and pencil, close your eyes, then bring down the pencil at random on the squares. Whatever square your pencil-point touches represents your stroke of the bat. When your first man is out, you play on until your team are out. Come, man, it really is interesting and will help kill this deadly waiting."

Recognising sound sense in this argument, Hamre took the book and pencil.

"To make it a dinkum game," said Pittendrigh, "I'll bet you a shilling a game."

"Right, but I haven't got a solitary shilling with me."

"I'll lend you one to start with. We'll both keep an account and settle up later at Alice Springs."

"Right!"

Hamre found the game surprisingly interesting. In the long days that followed it helped to pass many a forlorn hour.

That day they dined on one and a half tabloids. The three tins of meat were still intact. Weak from hunger, they lay down by the fire to face another bitter night. Hamre listened. Pittendrigh stared up at the stars and hummed, "Twinkle, twinkle little star!"

Next morning they lay in. There was no breakfast to get anyway. The cockatoos paid their early-morning visit and flopped heavily on the tree-tops, glaring down at the fire and screeching their raucous contempt. Those birds were rapidly getting on the men's nerves. In the full warmth of the sun Hamre stood up and walked off collecting stones, the birds watching him. He could not hit any of them, but he could at least annoy them. He got right under a tree and measured the distance to the lowest branch black with birds. He threw several times, with a long spell between each throw. Even that slight exertion made him gasp. The waning of his strength frightened him. He walked aimlessly off up the creek, drawn towards the camel-pad they had seen the previous day. A little farther along a man had scooped a hole that he and his animal might drink. Hamre stared down bitterly. To think that in this immensity a camel-man should come near them was a marvel; to think that in doing so he should miss their seventy-five miles of tracks by passing a few yards ahead of them was bitterness; but to think he had done so just when they were miles back searching for the tinned meats, was gall. Had they been in camp they would have heard him.

Hamre trudged back. Pittendrigh was bending over the fire with the acme of expectancy on his face. Hamre glanced curiously at the blackened meat-tin lid on the coals.

"Have one?" invited Pittendrigh.

"What?"

"Fried oysters!"

Hamre stared at the shrivelled things on the tin.

"Tadpoles!" exclaimed Pittendrigh, proudly.

Hamre laughed until he weakened and sat down. Pittendrigh lifted up the tin, only to drop it in the fire and swear vigorously at his burnt fingers. With two sticks he dragged the tin from the coals. With thumb and finger he secured a charred morsel and dubiously put the prize into his mouth. Then another and another in the endeavour to get a taste.

"How tall are you, Pitt?"

"Six feet in my socks – when I have any!"

"What do you weigh?"

"Ten stone here, fourteen in civilization!"

Hamre laughed again. "Six foot fourteen stone eating fried tadpoles!"

That day they ate one and a half tabloids, counting eleven left, with still the three tins of meat. Next morning, early, Hamre set out to walk to their only landmark, a little mound of a hill close to the camp. He was breathing heavily when he got there. The hill was a mass of rocks, hardly a hundred feet high. Hamre was exhausted when he climbed it. He stared out over the mulga tops stretching to a hazy horizon, then turned to the mountain range. Not a wisp of smoke, not a sign of bird or man in all the blue sky! He listened, his ears grown keen. Not a sound, save those wretched cockatoos away down by the creek.

Hamre turned to climb down lest the heat catch him before he could return to the shade – and abruptly stood still.

From the ground there stared up at him a big yellow-bellied goanna. It was fat! The thing knew Hamre's thoughts. He could tell that by the way his neck arched and the beady eyes watched him. He stared around for a stick, a stone. Not a missile was handy. He stepped stealthily forward. The goanna never moved. He stepped forward again, staring at the thing, trying to mesmerize it as perhaps it had mesmerized many a bird. He crept nearer, careful lest he trip.

He was just ready to pounce when it ran. He flung himself after it, clutching, trying to leap on it. It ran at a terrible speed, head high in the air, body erect on speedy legs, its tail twisting as it thrashed through the grass. It clattered into a crevice in the rocks, hissing venomously. Hamre snatched at the crevice, because he must snatch at something. He glared into the cleft and poked a stick into it. Then he sat on a rock and recovered.

It was New Year's Eve!

22. RESCUE

To celebrate New Year's Day a tin of sausages was to be opened. The two dined in state, ceremoniously preparing for the feast, conversing socially together as they sat with the tin between them. When they could stand it no longer they opened the tin and shook hands over it; and when the contents were shared they shouted and hurrahed. There was an extra sausage in the tin!

"There can't be much nutrient in the flies out here," said Pittendrigh. "Lack of vitamins or something!"

Hamre stared up disinterestedly. He was beginning to give up hope. "I don't think Joe will ever grow fat."

"Tom is brutally healthy," said Pittendrigh, "and lively on his pins. Did you see how he caught that one! He's got an appetite like a horse. But they don't seem to build him up at all. Still, his tail is a trifle more robust, don't you think?"

"No, I don't!" answered Hamre. He twisted and turned and grunted. "This wretched ground is getting harder every day. Isn't it awful?"

"Cheese it! Be British!"

"British be blowed! If your fat carcass was as thin as mine you'd have warts a foot long on your tail!"

"I'd still wag it. The lion never lies down."

"Rats!"

It had been a bitter night; they shivered over the fire until the sun rose.

"It is so easy to understand the abos now," sighed Pittendrigh. "Their eugenics are quite right, all squeezing into their gunyahs together, men, women, piccaninnies and dogs, all cuddling up for warmth. Thus they obtain sleep and keep the social fires burning."

"I can see you becoming a cave-man addict after this."

"Not on your life. Just set me down in Pitt Street once again, that's all!" Pittendrigh swore luridly as he crushed an ant in his trousers. "The 'bites' you get in Pitt Street are nothing to the double-barrelled nips out here!" he growled.

"Oh! oh! oh!"

"Oh, my fat aunt!" growled Pittendrigh savagely. "This sort of thing would make a saint swear. Look at my legs: once beautiful legs, now all red bites. And I'm dying for a bite. Look at those lizards, biting flies: and those cursed cockatoos and galahs and parrots biting nuts. Everything's biting something. And we can't get a bite to eat!"

"I'll tell you what," said Hamre slowly, "I've been thinking."

"You don't say!"

"Yes I have."

"Tell us the worst!"

"Well, I'll go and catch a lot of tadpoles. But you'll have to squeeze the bellies out of them!"

"I'll squeeze 'em," agreed Pittendrigh promptly. "What next?"

"Then I'll boil them. We might get a lot more out of them by boiling. When fried they shrivel up so."

Pittendrigh was already crawling out of the gunyah. "Come on, here goes for the great squeeze!"

From a puddle-hole rapidly drying up Hamre scooped a billycan full of tadpoles. It was a beastly job separating the green scum from the squirming mass of embryo frogs. Pittendrigh helped enthusiastically.

"Some of 'em have white bellies, some have black and some sport brown spots," he pointed out. "I wonder which will squeeze best!"

"For heaven's sake!" protested Hamre as he shook his fingers clear of the wriggling, slimy mess.

Pittendrigh "squeezed 'em." When the billy was filled with the awful-looking things he gazed on his handiwork.

"Flat as pancakes," he enthused. "My thumb prints on 'em suggest a new method for the C.I.D. 'Missing men traced by thumb prints on tadpoles'. 'Squeezed to Death on the Desert'. How's that for headlines for the 'Fishy News', Ham, old boy?"

Hamre boiled the things and they ate them.

That night they stared at one another as a whistling cloud sped by high up.

"Whistling ducks!" breathed Hamre. "Isn't it –"

"That's right," exploded Pittendrigh. "There's nothing would make me swear more tonight than hearing ducks fly past and not a duck to eat. But what are ducks doing out here in this God-forsaken hole?"

"Following the rains."

"Which is about the duckingest thing the ducking fools would do," growled Pittendrigh. "I wish one would fall and break his bleeding neck!"

"Wish in one hand –" began Hamre.

"And duck back with the other," finished Pittendrigh. "Yes, I know."

Next day they sprang from the gunyah, their hearts pounding. Through the air came a steady, humming drone. They shrieked and waved fragments of clothes. There, flying only 1500 feet above the ranges, soared two R.A.A.F. 'planes! They snatched firesticks and ran to the signal fires, hoping the 'planes would turn towards them. But the machines droned steadily on.

In exuberant delight the two assaulted another tin of sausages. Now they would be found! They devoured some milk tabloids as well: they were deliciously extravagant of food. Their shirts were sacrificed as signal flags on the gunyah. There was little sleep that night.

Next day was a day of waiting and longing. Towards evening there came a drone, rapidly growing into a metallic hum. The 'plane circled above them, promisingly low down. The men went frantic, shouting and waving. They must be seen. The 'plane droned away, fading into the west. They stared in alarm. What did it mean? Quite frightened, they decided not to eat at all. There were only one tin of pie and three milk tabloids left.

The following day they sighted a 'plane afar off: they could hear the faint humming as she droned towards Ilbilba. The flies were bad, the heat worse. The cockatoos chuckled in derision. The men scooped out a six-foot T in the red sand and filled it with white ashes from the fire. Surely that must be seen from the air! They were very weak now. Next day the sun rose all red above the MacDonnell Ranges: a hot wind raged over the bush. There was no sign of a 'plane. Then came the inevitable reaction. What if the 'planes never returned? They might regard this area of country as having been searched in vain!

The ration that day was half a tabloid each.

In the morning Hamre opened sunken eyes to stare unseeing at Pittendrigh, a rapt expression on his face. He was biting his lips; then he fell back with a groan. Pittendrigh leant over him.

"Pitt, old man," croaked the stricken Hamre, "I dreamt I was eating cheese sandwiches!"

Pittendrigh drew away in disgust. "I thought at least you were dying," he growled. "Cheese Grandmothers!"

Hamre leaned up and clutched him. "But, Pitt, such a wonderful dream, so absolute and convincing. A shower of cheese sandwiches rained down from the sky. Heavens, I can still taste them: I can *smell* them. Pitt, those sandwiches were *real!*"

Pittendrigh glared disgustedly. "Where the flamin' hell is my share then, you greedy guts!" he croaked, as he crawled away.

They got a pole from the creek and tied a rag to it. Hamre could barely drag himself about the camp; so Pittendrigh took the pole to the little hill and set it up. He returned to camp exhausted.

"Never again," he declared thickly, "will I be explorer on an empty belly. Yonder hill, upon which that noble flag waves, is henceforth and for all time Mount Pittendrigh. I have put my name on the map."

"A dashed inaccurate map!"

"What odds. Though the map may shift, Mount Pittendrigh will remain for ever."

"That is likely," said Hamre, ominously.

All they had that day was hot water. It tasted different.

Next morning they crawled about, enlarging their ground-sign; then opened their last tin of pie.

"No good them finding dead bodies," said Pittendrigh. "If they're going to find us at all it might as well be alive. If they don't find us soon it won't matter whether or no."

"We must try and last out," insisted Hamre huskily.

"The tadpoles are all done," said Pittendrigh, "and the mint. I believe those cursed lizards will seek us out."

"We're not dead yet."

"No, but we haven't a feather to fly with – yet."

"You'll make a lovely angel."

"Not while we have two tabloids left," answered Pittendrigh, decidedly.

The men lay there, listening as they talked in broken sentences, trying to persuade themselves that on two tabloids and grass they might last for another week and a day.

The water-supply did not bother them. The hole was drying up fast. They had measured day by day the evaporation rings around it and calculated that the water would last as long as the tabloids.

That evening Pittendrigh staggered to the creek for water. He tottered back, gasping, his eyes bulging.

"Ham, old man, quick. There are ducks by the waterhole!"

Hamre stared up, not comprehending.

"Ducks, Ham, ducks! Wild ducks!"

Hamre staggered to his feet. They sneaked down through the bushes and peered. There, at the edge of the fast-drying water, stood four wild ducks, two full-grown, one medium-sized, and a small young one. Hamre sank on his stomach among the bushes. Foot by foot he wriggled away to the right to get behind the ducks. These stood staring at the head of Pittendrigh glaring above the bushes.

An unearthly quiet was upon the bush. Even the cockatoos were quiet. Full-bellied, they were preparing for their evening flight home. Hamre, breathing in powdered grass, shivered when a dry stalk rasped across his ear. He lay perfectly still.

The ducks had not moved. They still stared at Pittendrigh, whose eyes were like saucers as he stared at the ducks and the apparition crawling up behind them.

As Hamre drew himself painfully forward upon his chest, inch by inch, the markings of the ducks stood out in beautiful metallic blues and greens. Lord, how plump the two big ones were! Now the ducks faced around. Hamre's heart missed a beat. Then the two big ducks stared at the baby duck. Hamre crawled forward. The little thing, held between those pairs of glaring eyes, was perturbed. It quacked protestingly. The hunter was very close, only three feet away. The duck, alarmed, looked all around and quacked a pleading, frightened note. It jerked its head towards Pittendrigh. Hamre plunged forward arms and body outflung. He just felt feathers as the duck, at lightning speed, dived into the bushes.

Hamre laid his head upon his arms.

Next morning the drone of 'planes overhead drew the men from the gunyah. They were too weak, too disheartened, to be overjoyed. It seemed the 'planes would never see them. What was the use of being overjoyed at sight of 'planes anyway? There were only two tabloids left.

But that afternoon there came a drone that grew into a roar as two 'planes flew towards the gunyah and swooped low overhead. The men danced drunkenly and yelled as arms waved in recognition from above. They staggered to snatch a message that came fluttering down: "Are you Pittendrigh? If so, lie on the ground. Where is your machine? Point in direction. Will drop food. Light fires to guide cars to you tonight. Eaton, R.A.A.F."

Then food rained down. The first tin almost fell on Hamre. He tore it open. It was full of cheese sandwiches! With a startled cry he rammed three in his mouth and wolfed them. They were saturated with benzine and engine oil!

But there were bags of good things and wonderful cigarettes. They ate – afraid to eat too much lest their weakened stomachs sicken. They smoked in between gorges. Then Hamre became violently sick. It seemed the last straw that when the cheese sandwiches came they should make him sick.

Then it was Pittendrigh's turn. "Oh Lord," he groaned, "an hour ago dying of starvation, we're dying of eat! I'm that stiff, that if I were to throw up a threepenny bit it would come down a brick and choke me!"

Beacon fires were kept burning all that night. They did not sleep – just sat by the fire, smoking in delight; casting longing glances at the food; taking a bite as often as they dared. They could spit, too! After such a famished time it was wonderful to spit on the coals and hear it sizzle! The next morning they were enjoying a quiet cigarette. The bush looked almost beautiful; the cockatoos called less derisively.

"Live and let live," quoth Pittendrigh, magnanimously, as he fed Tom and Joe on biscuit crumbs. "Grow fat and multiply."

A series of piercing yells startled them as clothed natives dashed down on the camp, and seizing the men's hands, shouted their surprise that they were still alive. Horses and camels sounded crashing through the mulga as from the bushes the huge form of Archie Giles appeared, his face wreathed in smiles. Pittendrigh swears that Giles's roar of greeting was the most thunderously welcome sound he had ever heard. The billy was put on, packs slung off, and Giles laid before them a great round of roast beef.

"Get it into you," he smiled; "it will make you feel prime." He sat down and carved and they ate. The billy was boiled five times.

Eaton had dropped a message to Giles three days previously, advising him that the search was narrowing down. Would he bring a ground-party in this direction? In four hours the big bushman had killed a bullock, loaded the team, and sent his natives far ahead to cut tracks. He had travelled night and day since then. Lieutenant Evans, of the R.A.A.F., landed soon after Giles's arrival. There was more hand-shaking; more delightful conversation. In the evening the car arrived with Government Resident Carrington, Dr Kirkland, and Colson. They had driven all through the night over roadless bush. Pittendrigh gazed unbelievingly as a flask came to light. He and Hamre each took a glass and smiled a silent toast to the other; the succeeding ones were not silent. The two men learned that it was Colson's camel that had passed within fifty yards of their gunyah on that day seemingly now so far away.

The party travelled back all through the night, Pittendrigh and Hamre too excited to sleep. A boisterous welcome awaited them at Alice Springs when the pitiable-looking scarecrows arrived. Each man had lost twenty-eight pounds in weight. The residents could not do enough for them.

"By the way, Ham, old boy," said Pittendrigh, confidentially, many hours later, "there is a little matter of a cricket score!"

"By Jove, yes! We'll settle up now."

They took out the tattered notebook and after arduous calculation found that Pittendrigh owed Hamre one shilling.

"But I lent you a shilling to play with," expostulated Pittendrigh.

"It's mine now," smiled Hamre. "Thanks!"

Immediately after they had reached Alice Springs, Dr Kirkland set out on a hundred-and-eighty-mile ride to save the life of a man suffering from a fractured skull. Such is life in the far out-back.

A rather strange fact that Hamre learned at Alice Springs was that his wife in Sydney had a strong presentiment he would be found alive just before the actual rescue. In her despair a "voice" had come to her and "told" her so. She had sung at her work for the rest of the day. Hamre could not help thinking of his vivid dream of the cheese sandwiches.

Colson left Alice Springs almost immediately with a new wing for one of the R.A.A.F. 'planes roped to his truck. While landing at Ilbilba the 'plane had smashed a wing against a grass-hidden stump. Pittendrigh's 'plane was not yet located; the R.A.A.F. 'planes were still searching for it.

Taylor, at Ilbilba, his mind relieved of one great anxiety, immediately began to worry over Lasseter. Where was the man? How was he faring?

Bob Buck.

23. LASSETER WITH THE BLACKS: THE EMU HUNT

For months, Lasseter lived in daily peril of his life. Watta Mitta Mitta from the first day they met had urged the tribesmen to kill him. Lasseter could only keep this man's active antagonism at bay by pandering to the collective appetite of the crowd, by studying each man and trying to win his friendship by flattery or admiration, according to the psychology of the individual concerned, and by securing what goodwill he could from the lubras by playing with their children. Above all, he studied "Old Bones", as he mentally called the witch-doctor, who in turn watched Lasseter as a cat watches a mouse. It was the witch-doctor's tacit consent to his presence that swayed the crowd in Lasseter's favour. "Old Bones" regarded him as an outcast and a liar, but a desperately cunning one, a useful one, who had enhanced his own prestige with the tribe.

Old Warts was Lasseter's one friend. He helped him right throughout. When Lasseter's real trials began, the old man would drift among the groups, throwing in a word here and there where it would do most good. Of this man, Lasseter wrote in one of his last letters: "If this is handed to a white man by an old man with a wart six inches long on his back, treat him kindly."

Lasseter had, next to Watta Mitta Mitta, most to fear from the young bucks. They were liable to turn on him the instant an unwary word or action of his nettled their sullen tempers. Any warrior who can boast he has speared a white man, is "sung" in tribal ceremonies for years afterwards. Watta Mitta Mitta, the big chief, warrior and hunter, badly wanted this boast sung to his name. Once, Lasseter jovially called the big chief "Micky", but the savage turned in such a fury that Lasseter kept the nickname to himself.

Lasseter was wary of the young lubras, giving no buck excuse for jealousy. But he always had a joke for the old women. The mothers' goodwill was gained by admiring the children. Lasseter whispered to each mother what a mighty warrior and hunter her son was growing to be. When the tribe got used to Lasseter, they accepted him. But as time dragged on and no great bird, no string of camels came, Watta Mitta Mitta jeered at his tribesmen as fools. At first, they gave Lasseter freely of their food. Later, they grudgingly threw him a bone as to a dog. He would have starved altogether had it not been for Old Warts.

Watta Mitta Mitta, the leader of the aboriginal tribe Lasseter was forced to join after his camels had bolted.

Often, in those wanderings, Lasseter thanked his lucky stars he had joined the tribe just at the close of a seasonal "wet". Game, grubs, lizards, beetles, snakes, rats, larvae, marsupial mice and edible fungus were plentiful. Grass-seeds and coarse shrub fruits, too, were abundant.

Had it not been for the first rough week, Lasseter would have acclimatized himself, memorized waterholes and those strips of country that grew the most plant-life, and been independent until succour arrived. But those first hot long marches between water-soaks, the scraps of goanna, lizards, yams, nuts and wallaby thrown on the coals and devoured almost raw was too sudden a trial for his untrained stomach. Presently dysentery left him yet more pathetically at the mercy of the tribe. He was travelling with a people whom stern necessity compels to kill or abandon their own sick. "They who cannot keep up fall out!" is the merciless law of the wild when the necessity for food compels the tribe to move on.

The tribe travelled in a big circle, keeping within the borders of their own territory. It was on the move now. Lasseter was hungry; all were hungry; no one had eaten the day before. They were moving up a narrow grass-covered valley, lined with trees, between two ranges.

Granite rock and ironstone were prominent; quartz "blows" gleamed like snow-caps on hilltops. Lasseter wished he had a chance to prospect that good-looking gold country. This band of savages might well be walking over millions. But they would value one fat goanna more than a ton of gold!

The cliffs hemming in the valley were actually two miles apart but the walls appeared barely a spear's throw away. In the sunlit valley the silence was broken by the ringing call of the bell-bird and the musical hooting of rock pigeons. From the mallee and kurrajong trees came a rowdy chatter of parakeets, while queer soughing of air-currents came from the valley top.

Scouts in twos, at signal distance apart, were spread from wall to wall of the valley. Lasseter, trudging hungrily beside Old Warts, hoped they would soon find something: it was a likely looking place. As keen as any native, he kept his eyes to the ground seeking tracks. He was meat hungry. He glanced behind. Only three lubras were in sight, squatting as they dug with their yam-sticks on a dry creek-bank.

Lasseter felt hungrily glad. The gins, anyway, were finding a few yams, roots and bulbs. They might knock a paddymelon with a yam-stick; that was their job. Behind them he knew were four warriors ready to raise the alarm and put up a running fight against any surprise. It was always possible that the main body might pass concealed enemy tribesmen who, when the dawdling lubras came along, would rush out, spear whom they could, and, snatching a couple of the younger lubras, rush them night and day back to their own country. On such occasions the captive women never hang back. Vicious prods in the buttocks from spear-points put speed into their pace.

A warning "Yo-ie!" sounded in front as a centre scout broke back from the bushes, his right arm high in the air, his hand and arm bent to the exact imitation of an emu's neck and head. He threw up both arms, then arched his back, standing side on while his emu arm bent down pecking grass.

"Two emus feeding," hissed Old Warts. The three lubras away back were already standing up as Warts turned and repeated the signal. These repeated it to others behind until, in minutes, the last straggling lubra had grabbed her pitchi, snatched up her baby, and was running to be in at the kill.

With panther-like strides and speed the main body raced up to the now-vanished scouts. Hardly the thump of a football sounded as some leaped away to the right and left to join those hurrying around the flanks. Mitta Mitta's crowd, with whom was Lasseter, converged on the two centre scouts, who, kneeling behind bushes, waved back caution. The big birds were presently in plain view, feeding unconcernedly towards them on a little grassy flat enclosed by bushes. Now began a long, silent wait while the ambush formed round the birds. As the lubras came panting up, the more agile dropped their burdens and disappeared to right and left to help close in the circle. Every walking child, the boys flourishing reed spears in almost hysterical excitement, took his or her place in the line.

The male emu, a fine big chap, lifted high his commanding head and listened, a picture of wild alertness. He lowered his head again, feeding, clucking reassuringly to his mate. She was the smaller bird and her drab brown feathers were commonplace beside the deeper black of her mate. Slowly they came on, with long stately steps, halting to peck a mouthful of grass or to stretch their long necks high in a bush and gobble a bunch of berries. Titbits were acknowledged by both in satisfied little duckings.

Presently, the male jerked up his head and twisting it around, stared in motionless alarm. Something had come to him through the air: there was no wind. The men behind must have drawn close for the emu to smell on a windless day like this. Partly reassured, the big bird fed on again but made a deep drumming noise, and the effect on his mate was instantly to make her more alert.

Six of Mitta's men, each stooping low as he held a thick bush before him, crept forward step by step. Both emus were now standing still, gazing uneasingly around, listening. The male bird, with his long neck stretched to its fullest height, had a commanding view high over the shrubbery. One could see the blue of his neck under the black, hair-like feathers. The emus awoke to a definite menace. The big bird wheeled to his right front, advancing a few steps, menacingly drumming. He had seen a bush move! As he stared at it another moved over there! His head turned instantly, but that bush was quite still. Ah, his mate had seen a bush move over here! They peered towards it, but it was only a bush. Ah, the big bird wheeled sideways for a bush moved in the wind and there was no wind! He did not understand it, these bushes that apparently moved to instantly stop. The smell of danger, too! But he could neither see nor hear it.

Thus the stalkers edged closer, holding the birds' attention while the rest stealthily closed the circle. The birds moved closer in companionship, clucking uneasily, ready to dash away. From a bush there arose an emu's head and neck, a strange emu. Surprising that the big bird had not seen it before, this emu clucked and hissed so warningly, and encouragingly beckoned the uneasy birds!

"Come straight on. It is all right here behind the bush!"

One could not but admire the "emu talk" of the hunter as both birds stepped towards that enticing neck and head swaying above the bush. It was the dried head and neck feathers of an emu around a warrior's arm, and he clucked "emu talk" to perfection. The birds came hesitantly towards the decoy, their long necks twisting from side to side.

There was a clicking as throwing arms twitched wommeras against spear butts. The big emu had come within spear throw before he realized he was betrayed. He halted instantly, his head thrown back, toes outspread, wrath in his poise. Before the birds could run, six bushes fell aside and six men stood there with poised spears. As the birds moved spears whistled and a concerted yell announced a ring of men, women, and children leaping forward to close in as they raced.

The emus dashed off, one with a spear swaying in its body. They swerved to a swaying of bushes as Mitta Mitta's crowd yelled right down upon them, hesitated one fatal second, then turned and raced back into men and women who were leaping towards them, the lubras shrieking as they hurled yam-sticks.

The circle had closed to half a spear throw between each man. The wounded hen crashed down kicking, with three spears in it. The big bird dashed straight on and caught the spear of the "emu-man" full in the breast. It leaped high to thump sprawling, churning the gravel, a target for twenty spears. The warriors rushed in, striking with their wommeras, leaping aside from those flail-like legs, striking at that dodging head which struck viciously back.

Lasseter danced with the others. Here was meat, plenty of meat!

24. BOB BUCK AND LASSETER

The directors in Sydney were worried men. They felt helpless too. All that money and forethought could do in striving to help their lone prospector had been done. And yet effort after effort had met with disaster. Their most careful plans relied entirely for success on the individual efforts of several men operating over two thousand miles away, under conditions and circumstances over which they had no control. The last letter from Lasseter, delivered by Johns to the Government Resident at Alice Springs, had described his location of the reef and given directions as to how a ground-party might follow him up. But for many weeks there had been no news from him nor of him.

Taylor returned to Alice Springs with Colson. The Defence 'planes had located the *Golden Quest* and the two men set out with Colson's truck to salvage it. They travelled by day and far into the night. The trip was finished on foot through heavy timber. The 'plane was found and a track cut through the mulga for the truck. Weather had played havoc with the external parts of the 'plane. There were holes in the wings; the elevators were warped and a front centre section cross-bracing wire was broken. Taylor looked glumly at this evidence of more work and delay. They dismantled the 'plane and brought it through the timber (a ticklish job) right to Alice Springs.

There, Taylor received urgent instructions from the directors to set out immediately with Johns and a camel team. Lasseter's directions were given. They were to pick up his tracks and follow them until they found him. A fortnight later, at Ilbilba, Taylor mustered his native acquaintances and sought news of the prospector. The natives shook their heads. They either knew nothing or would say nothing. Taylor and Johns packed up and started off, the black boys on ahead searching for Lasseter's tracks.

Tracks in the desert country last a surprising time. Camel-tracks have been known to last for years where no heavy rain had fallen and the tracks had not crossed loose wind-blown sand.

They had only been a few hours on the march when Taylor felt sharp pains across his back. By afternoon he was gripping the saddle, swaying with every stride of the camel. Camp was welcomed that night. Taylor was much alarmed, knowing only too well the symptoms of acute kidney trouble; he had been many months now drinking the water from native wells. He carried on all next day but at evening was seriously ill.

Next morning Johns turned the camel team back to Hermannsburg.

Arrived at the Mission after agonizing days, Taylor did the only thing he could do – made a proposition to Bob Buck of Tempe Downs Station that he should search for Lasseter. Taylor forwarded Lasseter's letter in which the prospector had indicated his future probable camps and described prominent landmarks where, under the ashes of campfires, he would bury letters.

Robert Buck has the reputation of being one of the finest bushmen in Centralia. He accepted the commission on behalf of the Company, and started out with his own camel team and natives on a trek that created a record for Australian tracking. For eleven weeks, and over hundreds of miles of unknown country, he tracked and at last found Lasseter.

When Taylor started for Ilbilba, Lasseter was living on rats. On his hands and knees he was staring at a dome-shaped nest in a tussock of grass. Old Wart's lubra was coming up behind the nest, yam-stick in hand, the light of battle in her eyes. A mother rat, pretty in her bright, fluffy brown fur, was in that cosy nest, her delicate ears twitching nervously, her little nose sniffing, her beady eyes shining with fear. Little baby rats cuddled warmly against her. She had all the responsibility, for the "old man" had cleared out. There were many such nests in this dry clump of mallee and spinifex. The furry desert rats were good eating and were caught simply enough. As Lasseter made a smack for his rat, the undergrowth in a spreading semi-circle burst into flames with a crackling that grew to a roar.

Black figures ran along the semi-circle trailing blazing grass, yelling as they ran. All ran to close up the one open part of the circle towards which the wind was rushing a wall of flame. Spears flew, yam-sticks whizzed, to ricochet thrumming just above the ground. Half-blinded by the smoke, in panic at the inferno roaring down behind them, three wallabies and a paddymelon came bounding for the open patch which was their only way of escape. Down went the wallabies, kicking, to the spears. But the little white-chested paddymelon, coming hell for leather with his ears back, ran the gauntlet and broke through to the howling remorse of the children. Scores of rats in singed terror came straight for the getaway, to be bowled in all directions by the yam-sticks. Lizards came scurrying; kangaroo mice came hopping on queer little legs; a brown snake hissed as he slithered for his life. Odd birds darted up from the smoke. Wheeling brown hawks swept down from above for the small fry. After the fire, the people ran back over the charred ground, hopping when a bare foot slipped down into a hole of glowing coals. There was great feeding on the ground – half-roasted rats and charred lizards in all directions. These morsels were seized and devoured as they were.

To better allocate the country and its game the tribe were hunting in families; three families hunted together. Later, at the coming of the moon, all the scattered families were to reunite. This particular group comprised Old Warts and his lubra, Gadgadgery, the Man-eater, with Lerilla his wife and their brood, Thurragerra, the Lousy one, with Miltijade his nagging wife and her brood, and Lasseter. He, grown gaunt and wolfish-looking, would have tried to make his way back to civilization alone but for his health; would have chanced Watta Mitta Mitta following him up and spearing him. Lasseter never gave up hope; he would still hopefully bury a letter in any prominent camp. His few ragged scraps of paper were guarded as if their value was far above gold.

In all his wanderings Lasseter looked keenly for Johns's tracks. If Johns carried out instructions, if any of the party carried out his instructions and made a base at Lake Christopher, then the tribe in its nomadic circle must cut the tracks – providing the relief party did not come after the tribe had passed. Sometimes he wondered if Johns had delivered those letters; but, again, he felt sure that he had. What had the directors done on receipt of them? If only they had sent an aeroplane! His bitter thought was that he had found a great gold reef, wealth untold, and yet it was not worth to him now the price of a pound of tea. He guarded one little scrap of paper very carefully: important news, in fewest words to the directors. Then "To my Dear Wife–"

This little family trip was a heartfelt relief: it separated him for a time from Watta Mitta Mitta and the witch-doctor. He dreaded the time when, soon, the nomads would band together again.

After the feed provided by the burning, the family group lazed their way to the "Valley of Sighs", where one night they camped. Desert oaks down in the flat, black pines high up in the gorges filled the valley with sighs as the wind whispered through their leaves. Clouds covered the sky. A tiny fire, shielded by a wind-break, glowed in the blackness of a rock-cleft. Old Warts's lubra, with half-closed eyes, swayed to and fro crooning some age-old song. Humpbacked, the light of memories in his eyes, Old Warts stared into the fire. Lerilla squatted by, suckling a dingo pup. Her husband Gadgadgery stared morosely at the coals, his ape-like features emphasized by his heavy, rounded shoulders. A night bird swished by. The cubs crouched a little closer to their wild parents. On a night like this the Spirits of the Night might seek rest in the bodies of humans. Little fists stealthily waved firesticks into a brighter glow, then passed the sticks over little bellies to keep them warm.

Miltijade was fire-hardening her new yam-stick. It was a solid stick of hardwood three feet long, both ends pointed for digging but one end thicker than the other. A good digging stick it would be, and a good thrower to break the leg of animal or wing of bird; a good club too to break the head of a rival lubra. Miltijade's eyes shone with the light of memory as she paid particular attention to hardening the club head. One does not forget a grudge easily when fathered in the wild. Thurragerra, her husband, squatted with a questioning frown upon his shaggy brow. He was busy. His tormentors had sought shelter in that thick hairy patch between his shoulder blades. He tried to reach them by holding a firestick over behind his shoulder; a whiff of singed hair came away in the breeze. Then Thurragerra burnt himself. He dropped back the stick and roared for Miltijade to come and scratch his back.

But Miltijade was busy with her yam-stick: she snapped at him to scratch his own back. He roared again and she snapped back, shrilling insults in a torrent to his answering roar. She goaded him to that point when she knew what was coming to her if she goaded a second longer. Then she dropped her stick and flew at his back, scratching with talon-like claws while shrieking in his ear.

Lasseter was sorry when the scratch was over. It had temporarily diverted him from his own dismal thoughts, fit companions in this "Valley of Sighs".

Gadgadgery snarled. There was the snarl of not-far-distant animal ancestors in that sound. Lerilla shrank away. She had put down the dingo pup and was giving her baby its turn. Gadgadgery considered she had not suckled the pup enough; he snarled again. But Lerilla with frightened eyes kept her baby at the breast. Gadgadgery sprang at her, striking savagely; she screamed, shielding the child. The man struck her again and again, wrenching at the child, but she doubled her body over the babe and screamed. Gadgadgery dragged her to the fire, seized a firestick and held it hard to the small of her back. Lerilla's screams rang down that Valley of Sighs. Burnt flesh tainted the air where only singed hair had smelt before.

Lasseter snatched Miltijade's yam-stick and brought the club down with all his strength on Gadgadgery's head. The savage spun around, loosening his grip on his woman. Another blow, across the right temple, the club sounding as if it had smacked wood, brought Gadgadgery with a grunt to his knees, mouth open and slobbering in wonderment. A third blow, across the left temple, and Gadgadgery sank to the ground.

Lasseter flung the stick from him, trembling in every limb. Any one blow would have killed a white man: the three had not killed this native. Lasseter had made another enemy. But he did not care – this was not a "thinking" enemy.

25. BAN BAN BALELE

Lasseter, so brown that he was nearly black, sat in the shade of a beautiful tree. Old Warts squatted close by, solemnly hardening a spear haft. Slowly he twirled the haft across his naked thigh and rubbed his rough palm backwards and forwards across it. The spear-head of hardwood on which the jagged bone barb would be gummed and bound rested in the ashes of the fire. Nearby were the lump of spinifex resin which he would heat and use for the gumming, the coil of kangaroo tendon for the binding, and his scraper of chipped quartz for paring down and scraping smooth the wood. A boy, who would be a great spearmaker himself one day, brought the old warrior a handful of coarse leaves from a rasp-like vine. These leaves Old Warts would use for the final polishing, just as civilized man uses sandpaper.

Now and again Warts would pull the haft out of the fire, squint along the wobbly stick, and with his hands straighten warp after warp. Then he would hold it out, poising it as if to throw. He was working in the exact balance needed to give it speed, distance, and trueness of flight when eventually it would be launched at the quarry. Thoughtfully he scratched himself as he worked the exact heat into the wood. A professor of chemistry conducting some intricate experiment could not have been more concentrated than he.

Their soak was in this big dry creek. Lovely trees shaded its banks for many miles. Wattle-birds, crested pigeons and parakeets sang their praise of the country. Opposite the camp a black ironstone bluff, bright with green quandong trees, overshadowed the creek.

Most of the bucks were out hunting, the old men and some of the lubras remained in camp. A group of lubras were roasting yams and wild onions under mounds of ashes, gossiping the while. Squatting with a flat stone between her thighs, a young woman shrilly talked while she cracked nuts. From a heap beside her she would pick a nut, drop it on the stone, and at the same time bring down her right hand holding the cracking stone. As her right arm was raised again she had another nut on the flat stone. She never missed a word or a crack in two solid hours. Those nuts had to be roasted, then ground to powder and washed to dissolve out a vegetable poison before the mash was ready for cooking as cakes on the coals.

A young boy came screeching down from the rocky bluff. He held a big wriggling lizard by the tail, and as he ran dashed it against a tree. The other kids stopped their spear-throwing and raced yelling to greet the conqueror. He tore through them, up to the old women, his eyes all excitement. Laughingly they congratulated him, loudly exclaiming what a mighty hunter he would become, urging the younger children to follow his example and go out tracking lizards. An old hag took the reptile, scraped out the coals with a yam-stick, and threw the thing on. It was still wriggling. As she covered it the legs stretched out convulsively through the ashes.

Lasseter was worried about his boots. How much longer would they last? There were other things too. He was recently recovered from an attack of dysentery, and the tribe were moving out tomorrow. He realized fully that he was a drag on this tribe. His boasted great bird did not come with those foods of his. Sullen looks greeted him wherever he moved. He still claimed his share of food as a right; he had to, or go without. This bluff was carried determinedly. Carefully he had saved his few remaining cartridges, hoping that when the end came he would get a chance to fight. Watta Mitta Mitta would be the first to go; *he* would stop a bullet exactly where Lasseter had showed him that evening long ago.

Lasseter looked up at the skies; he was now always looking and listening. What on earth had happened to Johns and Johannsen, and the 'plane and everybody? Why, he could be the only white man left in the world – the whole world could be dead and he never know.

That night the tribe squatted round a ring of camp-fires burning low. They had had good hunting in this district, and were going to celebrate with a little hunting-song and dance. They laughed and boasted as they rubbed their bodies with emu oil, smeared charcoal designs upon their chests and backs, bound circlets of grass round their limbs, fillets of feathers round their hair and parrots' plumage round their joints. Watta Mitta Mitta wore his eagle's feathers. Wedge-tailed eagle feathers are much prized, that bird being the hardest to kill.

The services of those men and women who were artists at decoration were in keen demand. Some men were great painters – they could mix vivid ochre that would stick on; and several of the women could grass a man in colours so that he looked like a bird.

The stamp of feet in the corroboree, the hisses and grunts were in rhythm to the wild chant of the lubras as they clattered wommeras and drummed their thighs. The boy piccaninnies gazed, their souls in their eyes, longing for the day when they too could dance as men.

These "play" songs and perfect mimicking of the recent hunts were more than boasting. The star actors in each play were the men who had killed game, and they danced to the killing in pantomime, extolling their every action. If these men had not been crafty and skilful in the hunt the tribe would have starved. It was their real life they were acting; an example to those growing up; glowing heroism to the children; a carefully thought-out scheme of men long ages dead to help preserve the race.

Lasseter wished they would stay longer in this district. There was still game about, though it was man-shy now. The tribe were "belly proud" and the curse of the wandering nomad was upon them. They were going straight out into the real desert now, Warts told him, to visit three distinct localities where a species of desert yam, very tasty and satisfying, grew plentifully and was ready for eating at this time of the year. After the rains the tribe expected a big harvest and they were now "yam hungry".

They marched in high spirits next morning, full-bellied and warm under a cheerful sun. That evening they camped at a soak on the edge of the sandhills country, nearing the fringe of the desert. The bucks during the day had speared only one wallaby. The women had dug fewer yams than expected. All were hungry and discontented after their good feeding of the previous few weeks. But as night settled down chants broke out from shadowy groups, laughter and crooning songs. They were crooning of the glorious feeds all would have when they got into the Desert of the Yams. They sang of previous trips, of the plentiful harvest so easy to dig, of how they ate and ate until even the skinniest man's belly swelled. Lasseter sat idly thinking. He wondered who had been the first to find this "soak" – a tiny hole dug in a sandy loam sheltered from the sun, draining, during the infrequent wets, water from the sand and storing it in this one tiny loamy spot with its thin band of holding clay. How craftily Nature had worked to supply the needs of these her youngest, and yet her oldest, children!

They pushed on all next day, crossing a sea of sand-ridges. Lasseter felt these sands were growing in his bones. He felt he had known for all time these stunted bushes growing yet more stunted and scarce.

That night he dined on half a goanna's tail, the long thin end with not a skerrick of meat on it; that was his share. He ate the meal slowly, carefully dusting off the charcoal, eating the singed skin, chewing the little bones into meal. When he finished, he only wished he had a dozen more such tail-ends to chew. He had to drink sparingly: there was no water here: there would be none until next night. From the last soak the lubras had carried water all day in their pitchis, with bushes over the pitchi to stop the sway of the water and the evaporation. No lubra had spilled a drop. Pity help her had she!

They pushed on next day very hungrily. Rolling red sandhills all day; not a wallaby, nor a lizard, nor a bird, nor a grub; not a yam, nor a root, nor a berry. Only ants and flies. At sunset they came to the crest of the last rolling sandhill. Lasseter gazed far out over a soft sea of gold with a crimson lighthouse beckoning them west. Lovely indeed, but it was "The Desert"!

At the foot of the last sand-ridge they camped and drank their last water from the pitchis.

Rapidly growing ravenous, the tribe set out next morning with the sand-ridges still shadowed behind them. The desert was a creamy expanse yellowing to gold as the sun shot up behind the human ants.

As they stepped on the desert proper, behind them a bell sounded, sweet, pure, and lingering. The liquid notes rang out again. "Ban ban balele"! The bell-bird seemed to be calling them back. Instant gloom settled on the tribe. The faces of the men grew stern; gossip died amongst the lubras; the children drew instinctively closer to their elders. Lasseter glanced interrogatively at Warts. What new superstition was this? But Warts shrugged and dropped his eyes to the desert sands.

The cool sand warmed with the morning; grew hot with the day; then the glare came. Straight on they trudged, only two scouts on ahead, a matter of habit really for this was "No Man's Land". The lubras and old people almost kept up with Watta Mitta Mitta's fighting men, for there were no yams to dig and the women, except those with very young babies, had no weights to carry.

Trudging on beside Old Warts, Lasseter again admired the youngsters, their childish brows turned down, lips doggedly shut, stepping silently on in the footsteps of their fathers. Human machines!

Lasseter felt pity for young Caby Yuro, so soon to become a mother. There were several others, too. In the middle of the day Old Warts pressed a little flat pebble into Lasseter's hand. Warts's thick lips showed a pebble as he grimaced. Lasseter sucked the pebble, hour after hour; it relieved thirst somewhat. Eyes to the ground, he watched his shadow grow less and less until it disappeared behind him. He set his mind to forget fatigue by fiercely concentrating on the meal he would eat that night. How he would gorge on those yams! Just like these hungry things, he would eat and eat. How true to nature they really were! Lasseter found that now, as on other occasions, concentration considerably deadened his present hunger.

In mid-afternoon there was a quickening of the pace. They were approaching the first yam-patch. How the sand sang under their feet! A silver tinkling in the silence. Deep grunts broke out, babes began to whimper. Almost at once the tribe smelled food, food! Lasseter shaded his eyes, staring for trees, a ridge, anything on the horizon to denote where the camping-ground might be. There was nothing. Presently his feet told him that the sand had changed to a compact brick red, as if mixed with loam: it looked almost "ground". Then came a light crackling, followed by a furious hunger at sight of the withered leaves of vines.

The lubras dropped everything, and, splitting into three groups, dug with yam-sticks. They dug down with amazing rapidity to moist earth. Soon the tribe clustered like flies around three tiny wells and drank deeply. Squatting there a few minutes, recovering, happy laughter broke out, piccaninnies rolled in the mud thrown out from the holes. As if by one accord the lubras arose and scattering wide across the dull-red ground commenced digging and rooting.

A low, wailing cry went up. The men leapt to their feet, staring as at a vision. Two kneeling lubras held up fragments like withered potatoes, the insides of which had been turned to red dust!

A dismal cry broke from all lips. The men ran to the other kneeling lubras, who were looking up listening with wild frightened faces. They dug feverishly. All the yams were blighted!

Kneeling, the tribe, piccaninnies and all, lifted their faces to the darkening sky and wailed again and again the notes that called them as they entered the desert: "Ban ban balele! Ban ban balele!"

Starlight on the desert that night was very lovely, very silent, very tragic.

26. THE DESERT OF THE YAMS

At dawn men, women and children filled themselves with water as a camel would. They must live on their own bodies and water. Lasseter drank slowly, long and deep, facing another day. This water was alkaline. Old Warts told him it was always so when the yams were blighted. That occurred rarely, about once in seven seasons. Even then there were nearly always sufficient partly-diseased yams to carry them to the next patch. But this time every yam was rotten, just dry red powder. From that alkaline water Lasseter dreaded a recurrence of dysentery.

As they pushed on into the desert again, Old Warts turned and pointed out the yam "country". It was a dull red strip of soil about half a mile long and a quarter wide, fenced with yellow sand.

In a guttural whisper, Warts told him of Ban ban balele. The bell-bird was a totem bird of this tribe. It warned them when the yams were withered. It had warned them before. Particularly it had warned them long ago, on one terrible occasion. That was why their tribe was so small now – Warts stopped abruptly and trudged on, glowering down at the sand.

Throughout that day they walked silently, fiercely, and by midday the old people were beginning to lag behind. Before sundown they came to the next patch of yams. These too were blighted.

That night Caby Yuro had her baby and it was knocked on the head. Lasseter, lying there in exhaustion, felt Old Warts edging something into his hand. Lasseter's fist closed on it with a terrible instinct. It was a wallaby bone covered in gristle, fire-baked a fortnight before. Lasseter turned over on his face lest they hear his teeth, lest they smell it! He gnawed that bone throughout the night, too famished to think of the strange affection of Old Warts, starving himself that the white outcast might live another day. The old man, stark naked, carrying only his spears, could not carry the bone. His old lubra had done so, hidden in her pitchi. The tendons of their legs would have been burned through and they would have been left to perish had they been found out.

Next morning the tribe rose as one to push on. Those who knew they must presently lag behind, dared not let the leaders get too much start. But two did not rise. Old Opperina and Wimmera crouched dumbly by the ashes of their fire. The tribe, a hundred yards away, stopped and looked back. Then all came back, spread out, and scraped up armfuls of withered vines – there was nothing else. They made up the last fire for old

Opperina and Wimmera. It would be too terrible for a man to die without his fire! The tribe departed without another backward glance.

That was a terrible day – unceasing exertion required on stomachs that had not known food for days. With bloodshot eyes the tribe walked on and on, urged ceaselessly forward by the indomitable will to live. Even those old ones who in ones and twos began before midday to drop behind, did not lag; their steps grew shorter almost imperceptibly, but they still followed to the limit of their individual will. Anyone who dropped would never rise again.

At midday the leaders slackened their pace, still keeping steadily on. The morning spurt had been accomplished and much ground covered. To sun and thirst, hunger and fatigue, would now be added the more dreaded enemy Despair! So the leaders slackened their pace only that the tribe might still keep together and fight against Despair.

Lasseter, staggering away behind with Old Warts, saw the day out. It was that day which eventually settled him. Just on sundown he staggered towards a forlorn mob, like sick cows, beaten to the ground. No need to read those bloodshot eyes. He knew! The third and last patch of yams was blighted. He swayed on his feet, the only one man standing, glaring at the pack as they glared at him. The tribe was done. Far in the desert, with a week of foodless wastes behind them, it was doubtful if even the strongest men would get back.

But Lasseter knew that the tribe must not, would not die. Individuals would perish, but the tribe must live on. How glad Lasseter was he had those cartridges! He must feed his tribe. Well, he would give them a feast. He gripped his revolver butt, and glared at Watta Mitta Mitta. The savage leapt up, his eyes blazing with fury. Lasseter pulled his revolver and laughed from blistered lips. He was going to die fighting! Gloatingly he levelled the weapon. The big chief stood, wommera half fitted to his spear, cowed by the certainty of death in those cold blue eyes. And the mothers shivered, trying with skinny arms to hide what plumpness remained in their babes. Whose child would be the first?

Old Bones crouched here, a grin on his death's-head face. Watta Mitta Mitta was afraid. Good! The witch-doctor's own position would become desperate immediately on the death of the white man. Only as long as this dingo lived could the witch-doctor attribute all misfortunes to that evil Kaditcha.

But Lasseter's finger warmed on the trigger. He would end it now; otherwise they would satisfy present hunger with a few babies, then kill him in the night while he slept. He steadied the revolver and–

A woman shrieked "Kamellie! Kamellie!" and they fell back, choking as she pointed. A sigh more poignant than any heard in cathedrals rose from the tribe. Coming to them, out of the sunset, was a giant camel!

The tribe divided, squirming to right and left like black snakes. With incredible rapidity those crawling horns spread out to encircle the oncoming beast. If only he would come within them! A wild camel, his desert instinct bringing him to this place. He would root the ground for water. The shadows came. With twilight the camel appeared huge and grotesque. Very slowly he came. He had halted but was coming on again. Even Lasseter knew the animal was sick. Lying with his chin in the sand, he spluttered in famished glee. The tribe would get that camel.

They did, and tore into the carcass like an animal pack, wolfing the raw flesh. Lasseter wolfed too, to quieten the gnawing demon inside him while he lit a fire of vines on which to throw his meat. He had not felt really hungry until he saw that pack savaging the carcass and had smelt the blood. Soon fires were lit. They would feast far into the night. Lasseter stopped himself from eating as soon as he could, fearful of dysentery. With meat beside him he lay by his fire, turning slices on the apology for coals, slowly returning from the shadow of death, wondering now at that miracle of a camel coming to them out of the desert. An eerie silence drew his glance towards the larger fire. A man there held up a little object. The rolling eyes of the whole tribe glared at those shaking fingers and at Lasseter. Suddenly he comprehended. He shrugged his shoulders and turned to his meat.

"When I pulled out the Kaditcha to kill Watta Mitta Mitta," he growled, "I told the spirit of the Desert to bring me my camel instead. For the tribe was hungry."

The tribesman by the fire held in his fingers a bullet from Lasseter's own revolver.

27. THE DEATH-BONE

After returning to their more fertile country, the tribe made a quick recovery. Not so Lasseter. His gorge of camel meat brought on dysentery again. He fought it and recovered, but was a very weakened man. And his chances rested on physical and mental fitness!

Sitting under a swamp oak, with a crowd of piccaninnies around him, he was fashioning a ball of clay and feathers. When sun baked it would roll better than their own balls, and when thrown through the air would flash with the colours of a flying parrot. He wove a checker board pattern of brilliant plumage into this magic ball.

Lasseter was weary with fighting the psychology of the whole tribe. What was that surly old wretch planning now? Squatting all alone as usual, like a scraggy crow in a trance, was the witch-doctor. The cunning mind was in no trance however. He was thinking that the white man's usefulness was finished; his presence now was a danger instead of a help to his own reputation. The witch-doctor thoroughly understood the inherent superstition of his tribesmen. He knew they believed the "Kaditcha" of the white man had brought the camel to them in their extremity. They discussed it with wonder and awe. Something must happen to the white man lest his Kaditcha finally overshadow the witch-doctor's reputation.

The day was beautiful, pleasantly warm, a sky of lightest blue with not a sign of wind. Visibility on such a day was perfect to a great distance. On a peaked hill were Old Bones, Watta Mitta Mitta and a group of the influential tribesmen. Lasseter was with them. They were preparing to "smoke-talk" with far-away tribes and Lasseter was in a fever of hope and dread at the result. They had "talked" before but had not got their signals beyond a certain radius. A tribe hemmed in by its neighbours cannot get its signals through if those neighbours are hostile, or for any other reason will not pass the signals on. Now, however, the "line" was clear; they could talk perhaps to far-away Ilbilba.

The "talk" fire was prepared of different species of twigs, wood, grass and branches. The signal ascended up into the air in an unwavering column of compact white smoke; it rose a surprising height before meeting an air-eddy which flattened its crest into a lazily drifting cloud.

The tribesmen squatted, the signallers stood, until from far away upon a far distant peak there arose a thin answering column. Eagle eyes saw it and grunts acknowledged it. The signal must be relayed, perhaps right to

Ilbilba, perhaps just so far out as the nearest tribe which had Ilbilba news.

In time, the answer signal shot up as a deep black column. The line was clear. The signallers immediately put an armful of bushes, flattened to shape, on their fire. The ascending column ceased. From the slow fire, smoke appeared. A signaller immediately thrashed downward with a bush and the smoke shot up in a perfect ring like an enormous life-belt, followed by a smaller ring which shot up through the larger. These were followed by another long ring and a quick short one until the addition of a different bush sent up a rolling black ring. Thus they talked; sometimes in uninterrupted column, sometimes in broken column, sometimes in corkscrew spiral, sometimes in a big spiral, occasionally in abrupt smoke puffs that flattened out and drifted as lazy clouds when high up. The smoke varied in colour, being white, grey, blue, black, according to the species of bushes used, or the heat of the fire, or the beating down on to the smoke as it was about to leave the fire.

Next day the answers began to rise, and Lasseter grew chilled at the deep, animal-like grunts around him. Yes, there had been big birds come to Ilbilba with white man's food. But the birds had all flown away. There were no white men at Ilbilba now. There were no kamellie loaded with white men's food coming through the land, not from there anyway.

Watta Mitta Mitta snarled contemptuously at his tribesmen as he harangued them on the way they had let the white dingo fool them. Simple fools, they had kept him on the fat of the land and would never get anything for it!

Angry exclamations, frowning brows answered the chief's accusations. Bones squatted there nodding his old head as he stared across at Lasseter. His face plainly said "I told you so"!

Lasseter knew it was best not to answer at present. They were all waiting: they would batter him at a word. That evening, when walking through the camp, his heart thumped to the hum of an aeroplane, the exact imitation of what he had taught the kids. He wheeled round on the mimicking little devils. Ribald laughter encored their efforts; it seemed that Watta Mitta Mitta would kill himself laughing. Lasseter felt sick. But next day he felt worse when he wheeled to a sharp sting in his leg. There were the children, toy spears raised, snarling like a pack of wolf cubs. He sought instantly to placate them, to divert their attention by some new game lest those elder children join in with the cubs.

A week later the tribe in their march halted to point at the ground and talk. There were the tracks of Lasseter's camels, quite plain, made months before; it seemed years to him. He stared around, recognizing landmarks. Why, they must be quite near Winter's Glen, the tribe had completely encircled their country. As they walked on, Lasseter's mind dwelt on the Glen. There was food and water there; he could find it himself now. But he felt very sick. With a fainting of the head he realized he was utterly dependent on these people for the few roots and scraps of meat they might throw him. When would Johns, when would Taylor, when would someone come?

A howl from behind brought the tribe all "Yack-ai-ing" back through the timber. Delight was in that cry that echoed from tree to tree. A call to a feast of honey-ants put speed into every leg. The lubras were scattered around the mulga trunks, shouting sallies to one another as to how it was really the women who always found the good food. But there was annoyance in their laughter and swearing from the men when they found that others were before them. Swarms of the tiniest ants, hurrying along the tiniest paths, all pouring into those little holes that went down among the roots of the mulga, aggressive little pirates, had located the store chambers down below and were very busy milking the honey-ants. In animal-like rage the men and piccaninnies stamped their feet upon those countless numbers.

Carefully the lubras dug, each following the tiny hole that went from two to four feet right down into the earth. Then it chambered out into many galleries and tunnels. Here were the honey-ants, delicacy of delicacies. Only odd ones were honey-reservoirs, utterly helpless creatures, their abdomens swollen like marbles with months' accumulation of honey. The busy workers gorge them thus, and keep them as storehouses to be "tapped" when hard times come.

Old Warts's lubra threw him a honey-ant and Warts handed it to Lasseter. The honey was visible as a golden fluid in the distended abdomen. Lasseter took the insect by the head, inserted the reservoir into his mouth and squeezed. A taste of formic acid was instantly overwhelmed by a flood of delicious honey. Lasseter reached out for more.

A few nights later the tribe camped in the "Valley of Caves". The cliffs of this sombre gorge were honey-combed with caverns. Several of them could have comfortably housed a line of omnibuses. In the camp cave the roof and walls, under the firelight, showed the crude drawings of a prehistoric art gallery – figures of giant birds and reptiles, of fighting men and of women. Churinga and totem drawings were in coloured ochre; others were in charcoal. Some of these faded pictures must have been done in the days when the human race was young. The tribesmen believed there were many spirit tribesmen with them in the cave.

In happy mood the natives sang, the fire glow throwing their wild shadows on the walls among the wilder pictures. Several tribesmen gave an exhibition of shadow-throwing – imitating an emu hunt, the stalking of a kangaroo, then the quick action of a savage fight, to the plaudits of the elders and intense interest of the children. They showed the stealing of a young lubra and her screams rang through the cave as they played. She joined in the spirit of the play, this wild young thing, her eyes fairly starting from her head, her breasts heaving in the shadow on the wall. Her screams were a thrill as her lover bounded up and thrust his spear deep into the belly of the woman-stealer. So has stone-age man long antedated the moving-picture show.

They were singing a battle song of the days when their tribe was numerous and fierce, dreaded in the land. The cave rang to the cymbal-like clash of wommeras, drummed hollowly to the clapping of the lubras, whose wild chant and wilder eyes urged the young bucks to leap to their feet and, seizing weapons, dance to the maddening song.

Lasseter, unwell and annoyed by the noise, quietly slipped from the cave, seeking peace and quietness. He would sleep somewhere all by himself. Outside, the valley centre was flooded in moonlight emphasized by the pitch black of the cliffs. Trees appeared as if their leaves were outlined in silver; grotesque shadows from towering rock-masses sprawled out in the valley.

Lasseter sank down on a soft bed of couch grass near a circle of bushes and lay staring wearily up at the stars. Presently he became aware of a hissing, low crooning hiss. Something in that sound made his blood run cold. Rising stealthily on his elbow, he listened. The hissing came from deep within the bushes. It was the witch-doctor, up to some devil's work. Lasseter crept through the bushes towards the sound.

On a circle of grassy sward knelt Bones, Watta Mitta Mitta, and two old warriors of the tribe. The witch-doctor, crooning and swaying on his squatting haunches, held a long, sharp-pointed bone in the direction of the cave. The other three men, squatting at intervals behind him, held clear of the ground a twelve-foot cord of human hair attached to the bone. The last man gingerly held a bone cylinder in which the end of the cord was fastened. Needle and cylinder had been carved from the shin-bone of a man. The performers swayed to the movements of the witch-doctor and hissed to the croon of his song. They were pointing the Bone, singing someone to death. The words of the insinuating croon, speeded in the direction pointed by the Bone by diabolical agency, were supposed to have the power of taking a little blood from the victim and, drawing it invisibly through space to the Bone, sucking it along the cord into the bone receptacle. Presently the bone-pointer would be reinserted in the cylinder, the cord carefully wrapped around it, and all sealed up with spinifex gum. The doctor, thus having possession of the victim's life-blood, could poison the victim through it, with disease.

Lasseter crept away. Unaccountably he sensed that the witch-doctor knew he was there. He walked slowly back to the cave. Who was it being sung to die? Who was it that had offended the sorcerer? Any Australian aboriginal at whom the Bone is pointed will surely die. The strongest arguments of civilization, ridicule, medicine, avail nothing against that deep-rooted superstition. Lasseter thought of Old Warts, his only friend. He quickened his pace at the alarming possibility. What if Warts was chosen to die?

Warts was in the cave when he got back. In heart-felt relief Lasseter squatted beside the old man, feeling as we all do towards a friend whom we have nearly lost. He lay awake all night, listening, glaring into the dark of the cave, shivering in the tension to smash any crawling shadow that might whisper into the ear of Warts–

"The Bone! – has been pointed – at You!" That was how it was done – the victim "dreamed" his death. Before dawn he leant over Warts. The smellful old heathen was snoring dreadfully. Lasseter lay back with intense relief, hardly conscious of the huddled forms of men, women and children, the animal-like snores.

The next few days were quite normal in camp. Lasseter kept close to Warts. He would ward off the poisoned words as long as possible. The more he thought of it the surer he was that Warts had been "boned". He never left the old man's side lest some treacherous emissary should approach and whisper:

"Have you an enemy?"

"No."

"Ah!" The look, the interchanging looks, and the confirmatory nod as the emissary crept away, would have been enough.

A week later, Lasseter was definitely sure. All the tribe knew. The only man who did not know was the man who had been "boned".

A quietness prevailed in camp; veiled looks and suggestive whisperings were directed towards the two men who sat a little apart. Even the piccaninnies knew; he saw it in their actions, their eyes. In despair he kept by Warts's side day and night striving to keep him constantly interested lest he notice.

It was the sorrowful look in Warts's eyes, the sad farewell from a man who cared that told the truth. Lasseter stared at the bowed back of the old man as he walked away.

The Bone had been pointed at Lasseter!

28. LASSETER'S END

Lasseter was speechlessly angry. That natives should have dared bone a white man! He glared around. The tribe sat in a strange silence – Lasseter knew that Kaditcha silence. "Ban-ban ba-le-le" tinkled his bell from far away. Warts had hurt Lasseter most. Warts, who believed his white friend was doomed!

In ones and twos the men stood up to drift away to their hunting. The women followed to their yam-digging, talking low-voiced. The children trailed after them, with backward glances at the sitting man. Already he was looked on as dead.

Lasseter was as weak as a kitten. With a furious anger at his own thoughts he hobbled from the camp. How utterly absurd that in these modern days stone-age natives actually thought they could kill a civilized man by superstition! He would show these black swine that a white man would not lie down and die as easily as they. He walked on and on, until suddenly he felt his weakness tenfold. He realized that they would not feed him now.

Why waste food on a man doomed to die?

A few days afterwards Lasseter awoke with sandy blight – almost blind. For the first time he nearly gave up hope. He began to write: little letters with a chapter in each line. He determined to make one last attempt: he would crawl back to Winter's Glen; rest there; then crawl on his old camel tracks to Ilbilba! One line at the foot of a letter describes the attempt: "Could not make the Glen, too weak–"

When Bob Buck reached Ilbilba he found the natives morosely uncommunicative. They denied any knowledge of Lasseter. So Buck commenced his search aided by Lasseter's guiding letter, written long ago to the directors. In the Petermann Ranges, over a hundred miles away, he found Lasseter's tracks – the tracks of a dead man, so a band of wild warriors assured him. The tracks vanished, and so did the warriors.

Buck found the tracks again another twelve miles farther on. Again the blurred footprints vanished, to reappear another ten miles farther ahead, deeply impressed in clay. Then tracks were found, strangely enough, at ten mile intervals, until they vanished in the sands of Gibson's Desert.

In crossing that desert Buck and his camels and natives came within an ace of perishing. They pulled through with half a gallon of water to spare; the camels went nine days without water!

After a spell to recover, Buck sent his native boys ahead again scouring the country. Eventually they cut a faint trail, the imprints sunbaked. Soon they were blotted out where a dust-storm had swirled over the land. But it was enough. Buck had the direction again. So the search dragged on until, one sunlit day, a loud cry from the scouting boys in front told of a find. The remains of a packsaddle lay on the sand! Nearby was a broken case and many blurred tracks still plain to the black boys' eyes. Buck searched in the ashes of a long-dead fire – in vain. The straw from the rotting saddle caught his eye. He pulled the straw to pieces and found a hurriedly scrawled note on a piece of tattered paper, the writing almost illegible. In a few words Lasseter told of the camels bolting, adding: "Dig ten feet from fire." Buck dug, and found what he had expected, for his boys pointed out to him where wild natives had dug before. A boy came hulloaing down from a sandridge:

"Tree up there got him brand!"

Buck climbed up. On the tree butt was roughly chopped "Dig five feet", and a broad arrow. Buck measured five feet from the arrow and unearthed an empty lolly tin. Paper apparently had been in it but weather and ants and rust had eaten the paper away. Eventually good information – two long letters in a corked bottle – was dug up. These described the locality of the reef and the natives, and gave much other information.

So Buck carried on, slowly, with the dogged persistence of his own camels. The trail led him to the natives' main camp. They bolted. He tracked them for thirty-two miles, and found them sullenly waiting. The scattered bands had joined up: Buck counted one hundred and ninety-seven individuals, then let the count go. He computed the Petermann crowd alone at five hundred. They knew nothing of any white man. They were "no liars"! Buck explained that they were liars and gave definite reasons for his belief. Unconcernedly he camped. He and his boys were well armed and ready for a show-down if necessary. At three in the morning a black boy stealthily woke Buck. An old man had crawled into camp.

"Him say white feller he die," whispered the boy. "Him want you to go now, he show you".

"Oh, well," yawned Buck as he rolled over, "if he is dead it is no good me going now. And I'm not walking out in the dark to be a pincushion for spears anyway. Hold him until morning. Tell him I'll give him a tomahawk when he shows me where the white feller is."

In the morning the natives clustered a little way off. Some lubras among them wore bellybands and hair ornaments, at which Buck stared.

"Heavens," he said to his head boy. "Poor old Harry! They've dug up

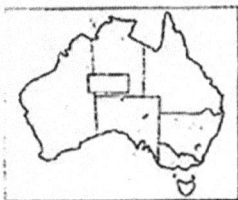

5   The main party reaches its farthest point west, Mt Marjory, in mid-August

6   In *Golden Quest II*, Lasseter is taken on a two-hour reconnaissance flight south-west from Ilbilba

7   The Thornycroft pushes south-west but is halted by rugged, sandy terrain

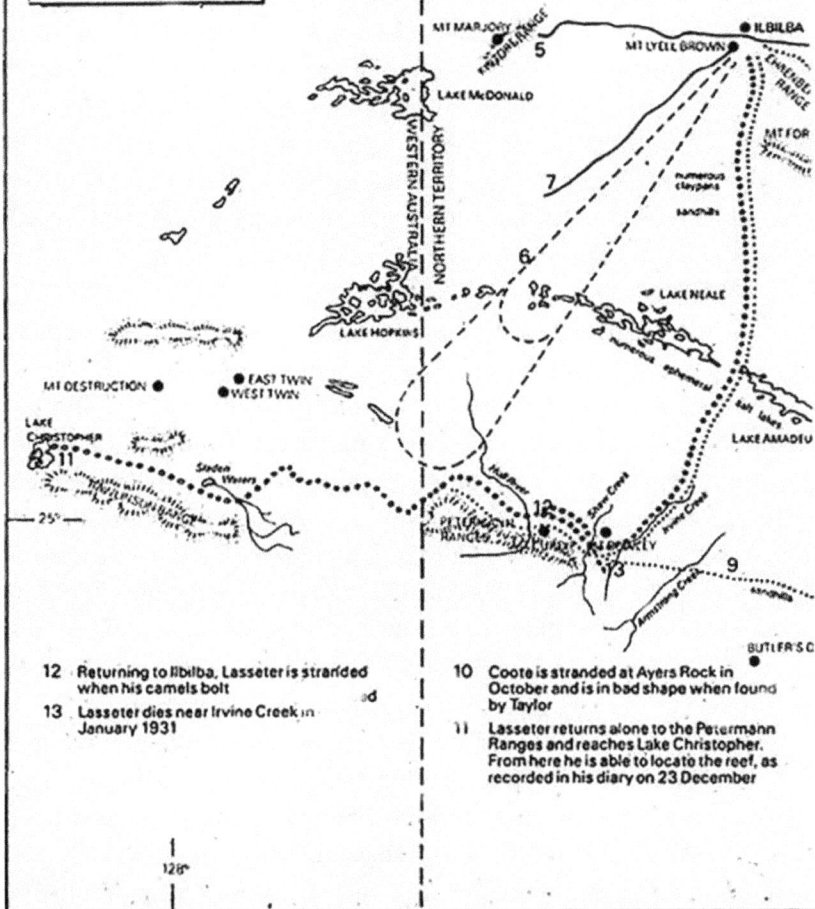

12 Returning to Ilbilba, Lasseter is stranded when his camels bolt

13 Lasseter dies near Irvine Creek in January 1931

10 Coote is stranded at Ayers Rock in October and is in bad shape when found by Taylor

11 Lasseter returns alone to the Petermann Ranges and reaches Lake Christopher. From here he is able to locate the reef, as recorded in his diary on 23 December

MT MARJORY RANGE
ILBILBA
MT LYELL BROWN
LAKE McDONALD
WESTERN AUSTRALIA
NORTHERN TERRITORY
EHRENBERG RANGE
MT FOR
numerous claypans
sandhills
LAKE NEALE
numerous ephemeral
LAKE HOPKINS
MT DESTRUCTION
EAST TWIN
WEST TWIN
salt lakes
LAKE AMADEUS
LAKE CHRISTOPHER
Sladen Waters
PETERMANN RANGES
Hull River
Stuart Creek
Anne Creek
Armstrong Creek
sandhills
BUTLER'S C
25°
128°

3 At Dashwood Creek fresh water is located and an airstrip cleared. Pittendrigh and Hamre make a forced landing nearby in December and nearly die

4 In mid-August Coote crashes on take-off at Taylor's Creek and the *Golden Quest* is wrecked

1 Expedition leaves Alice Springs on 21 July 1930

2 Micky, an Aboriginal guide, is recruited from Archie Giles near Hamilton Downs

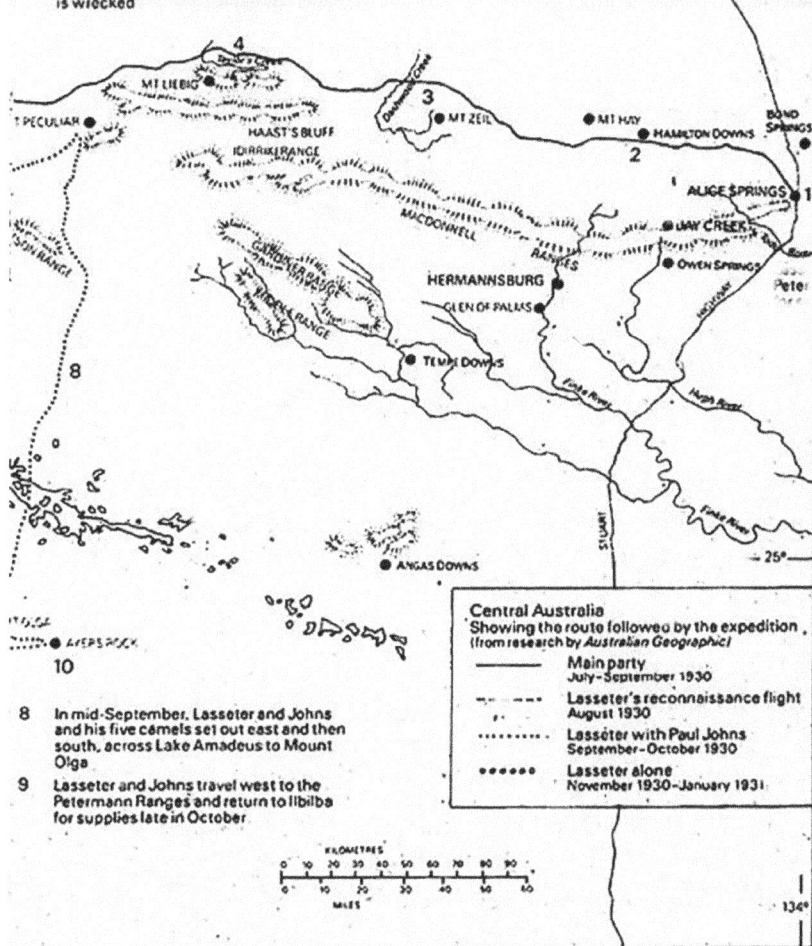

— 23°

T PECULIAR

MT LIEBIG

HAAST'S BLUFF

IDIRRIKE RANGE

MT ZEIL

MT HAY

HAMILTON DOWNS

BOND SPRINGS

ALICE SPRINGS 1

JAY CREEK

MACDONNELL RANGES

GARDINER RANGE

KRICHAUFF RANGE

HERMANNSBURG

GLEN OF PALMS

OWEN SPRINGS

Peter

TEMPE DOWNS

Finke River

Hugh River

STUART

8

ANGAS DOWNS

— 25°

Finke River

AYERS ROCK

10

8 In mid-September, Lasseter and Johns and his five camels set out east and then south, across Lake Amadeus to Mount Olga

9 Lasseter and Johns travel west to the Petermann Ranges and return to Ilbilba for supplies late in October

Central Australia
Showing the route followed by the expedition
(from research by *Australian Geographic*)

Main party
July–September 1930

Lasseter's reconnaissance flight
August 1930

Lasseter with Paul Johns
September–October 1930

Lasseter alone
November 1930–January 1931

KILOMETRES
0 10 20 30 40 50 60 70 80 90

MILES
0 10 20 30 40 50 60

134°

his photos and are wearing the films for bellybands!"

A band of natives guided Buck to where Lasseter lay under a canopy of dried bushes, his false teeth on the ground beside him. They had served him well, for he had used them as Kaditcha. Buck scratched his head thoughtfully.

"The natives would never dare touch those teeth," he said, "but it beats me why the crows haven't carried them away."

The boy nodded.

"By Jove!" exclaimed Buck as he turned over that withered canopy, "here's a lucky find – the nosepeg of the camel he grabbed when the brute bolted. It'll just replace that nosepeg old Rowdy broke this morning. Lasseter must have hung on well to have pulled the ring right out of the nose!"

An empty revolver and the tattered remains of a ground-sheet also lay beside the body. Buck dug in the ashes of fires and found letters, the last ones on scraps of faded paper, torn and dirty, written by the failing hand of an almost blind man. Words, sometimes whole lines, in those letters are missing.

Buck buried him, fenced him in; and carved the name of Lasseter on a big old gum-tree half a chain from the grave on the nor'-west side.

"He died in a pretty hard place," said Buck, "a rough place, right in the Petermann Ranges. He had stiff luck, because he nearly pulled through."

Scrawled on the back of his small son's childish letters, he had written:

They have made no ... to build me a ... anything for shade ... 78th day no ... food I realize my end is ... I also realize ha ... the appeal I ... s ... blacks from the ... can't see, nearly blind ... about the body sp ... held with all speed ... a packhorse or riding ...

Might have got to ... what hurts me ... not to know why I ... am abandoned thus ... weak to stand and have some ...... dysentery that will fin ...

... day the treacherous ... Watta Mitta Mitta ... big revolver he should ... a warning. If it were ... n I could have got ... he is now dragging ... ward ward for some ... too weak to ...... thout assistance ... to his arm round me ... dragged me five ...... lying on the ... rek where they ...... one old woman ... feed of ripe figs ... so I'm done for.

Lasseter is dead. Two prospectors who set out on his tracks are dead.

But Lasseter's dream lives. A big expedition has already been formed to carry on where he left off. His spirit will watch the dream come true.

29. THE SECOND ATTEMPT

Members of the second expedition that attempted to locate Lasseter's reef, on returning to civilization, report having failed by sixty miles to reach their objective. Apparently the hoodoo which pursued the first expedition was present here too, as although the party suffered no hardships, lack of foodstuffs forced them to return. Such lack cannot be laid to the Company's door, as an open cheque was given for the purchase of supplies.

When well on the route, the second expedition were surprised to see the pegs of a mining claim, and traces of prospecting work. It was a pegged out reef, and the prospector of the party was surprised to read the names of Harold Wilkinson and Mick Roach of Kalgoorlie, men he knew, on the pegs.

The expedition reached Lasseter's grave, a long way from the Western Australian border, and then returned.

The country over which the seekers travelled was practically all grassed, Bob Buck avoiding the desert patches across which he did such a notable tracking trip when seeking Lasseter last year. Several members of the expedition, with a knowledge of grazing country, report areas of the country passed over as being "well-grassed country". Most of the country, however, was coarsely grassed, though there was no lack of water, so far as water for camel-travelling purposes goes. They visited a number of fairly large waterholes. The natives told them of others; and fairly frequently showed them, by digging, water only a couple of feet underground.

The country, seldom monotonous, was always "wild" with at times a rugged beauty. Numerous bands of natives were met with, all stone-age men, few of whom except "Lasseter's tribe" had seen a white man before.

One tribe ran from them shrieking "Kaditcha! Kaditcha!" (the devil! the devil!), which was not too complimentary to our white skin and personality.

The moving-picture man with the expedition achieved something; with the result that some intimate pictures of these age-old men and striking scenery may shortly be on the screen. The film is unique, the first of its kind to be "shot" in the world. Unfortunately, its "nakedness" may bar it with the censor.

As to mineral possibilities of the country gone over, the only prospector of the party reports one considerable area of country as being "very likely looking", outcrops of quartz and ironstone running for miles. "It would take a strongly organized company years to systematically prospect this particular area," he states.

The location of this country justifies the Company's hopes. It originally equipped both expeditions, not only for the search for Lasseter's reef, but also with the well-thought-out belief that mineral-bearing country might be met with other than "Lasseter's country". It is a pity that the second expedition was unable to prospect, as the possibility, even, of an addition to Australia's mineral wealth at the present time would be of untold value. The geologists to the expedition however, so far as I am aware, report the country as being distinctly unpromising and definitely non-auriferous. The prospector returned to civilization with a lump of quartz to prove his contention of mineralogical country passed over, but in view of the geologists' unfavourable comments, the directors of the Company in their disappointment did not attach any importance to this. Recently, however, they sent the stone to Port Kembla for assay, and were surprised at a return of sixteen grains of gold per ton. Sixteen grains of course is worthless from a working standpoint, but the assay definitely proves that that particular quartz country is auriferous, and may hold stone carrying ounces to the ton instead of grains.

A piece of stone, also brought back by the party, is showing pyrites, "new-chum" gold. It was suggested that Lasseter may have mistaken the pyrites for gold. That, in my opinion, is unfair to Lasseter, who for some years worked on the rich Coolgardie and Kalgoorlie goldfields where he saw gold in the alluvial, in reef, and in bullion. His father (still living) is a prospector with a lifetime's experience and taught young Lasseter quite a lot about gold at a very early age. Again, far from casting discredit on Lasseter's assertion, pyrites is actually a favourable indication of gold. I do not think there is a goldfield in Australia in which pyrites is not present.

The map of the quartz blow, which Lasseter wrote was carrying his rich reef, and which he buried on the sandhills where the camels bolted was not located. But an empty treacle-tin, tightly lidded, was found buried deep near a tree on which was marked "DIG 5 FEET". Some photos, which he had buried nearby, were dug up by the natives, as related in an earlier chapter of this book. And the remains of his diary were unearthed in a cave, from beneath the ashes of a long-dead fire. The diary (incomplete) was written in a red-covered notebook, and a smaller notebook which had been tightly rolled so as to fit into an Oxo tin. The outer leaves are easily readable, but the warmth of the fire nearby, weather, and white ants have so damaged the tightly rolled inner pages that they break apart, and some fall in dust, when unrolled. The legible extracts, given in the next chapter, tell a story of dogged perseverance, of hope achieved, of hope deferred, and finally of hope lost during a desperate struggle for life. Where it has been possible to so arrange them, the pages appear in their original sequence.

The remarkable Lourdes water incident is explained by Mrs Lasseter, to whom my thanks are due for permission to print these leaves from the heart of a man who has gone. Mrs O'Brien, a life-long friend of the family, on the eve of his departure on his ill-fated expedition, gave him a little bottle of Lourdes water, saying, "Take this Harry, it will bring you luck. It is only a tiny bottle and you can carry it easily."

While Lasseter was existing among the natives, and praying for the relief which never came, he, of course, was unaware of the disaster to Coote at Ayers Rock, of the forced landing of Pittendrigh and Hamre, and of the last attempts at succour made by Taylor and Johns. When he felt his "abandonment" most keenly, he never quite gave up hope that Johannsen would come – little knowing that that strange "hoodoo" had already marked out Johannsen and his mate to be speared by the blacks in the Rawlinson Range.

In his little red-covered notebook are a few rather pathetic drawings, a relic of his many attempts to amuse the blacks at critical periods and divert their ever dangerous attention from him. At times his life rested on the "turn of a straw". There are drawings of blacks and emus, of kangaroo-spearers, hunters, piccaninnies and other objects of interest to native life. There is a quite recognizable drawing, too, of Old Warts, his only friend.

With his usual thoroughness, he had written out a "dictionary" of the language, with the English words opposite. But there are only a few words left.

In the red notebook, which is perfectly preserved, there are only twenty-nine pages. Lasseter had torn out seven to complete the diary in the tin, the paper of which is quite different to that in the red notebook. It had been a large notebook of quite one hundred pages. No letters recovered by either expedition (so far as I have seen) are written on the same paper as that torn from the red notebook. Hence, there probably are other letters somewhere, written on the missing sheets.

On page 238 of his diary Lasseter writes that he buried films in the top end of the cave. This was after he had discovered that natives (as described in the book) had dug others of his films up. Probably the men of the second expedition did not read the diary carefully as they did not search for these films, although successful in digging the diary from the cave. Seeing the natives did not find the diary it is highly probable that the films mentioned are still there.

In the last letter to his wife, found on his body by Robert Buck (on his earlier tracking trip) Lasseter states, after describing that he pegged the reef and photographed the datum peg (the "key" peg of a mining-claim or lease) – "I made the run in five days." This possibly means that the reef is five days' camel-ride away from where his body was found. The reader will notice that page 238 of the diary confirms Lasseter's statement in his last letter to his wife in which he refers to the known locality "where the camels bolted".

That the reef is five days from his resting-place, is deduced from a close study of this story, the letters, and the diary. If the reader himself will study them he will realize how the inner story gripped the writer and will grip him.

A marked tree led to the discovery of this later diary. Perhaps coming expeditions will unearth yet other fragments of the story – fragments that may lead at last to the unearthing of Lasseter's reef. Death has failed to write – finis.

30. DEATHLESS PAGES

(Fragments of Lasseter's diary and letters to his wife.)

... a brons ..... pigeons have just flown up from the ... water hole so I know the blacks are round somewhere the pigeons make such a whirr with their wings ...

Darling there is so ...... lot. I would like to say ... to you but I can't write ... it where anyone might re ... I've tried to make you happy and ... company ...... you .. u ...... be rich.

... the reef is a bonanza and to think that if only .... been guided by me we could ..... have got ..... truck .... in three ... p ... damnable that ....

.. later an old chap with a wart 6 inches by 3 inches on his back took pity on me ..... brought me some berries like cape gooseberries.

To my way of thinking this is the ninth day after the camels bolted .. and I photographed the datum peg dated 23rd Dec. ......

I can't understand ..... support or relief has not be ... afforded me. I wrote Edwards and also asked Carrington ... the Govt. Resident, to send word to the Company to sen ... me rein ..... they did not fu ... we with a ... consolidated ... ners right .... but expect .... t .... pe .... square .... enty ..... 28 acre r .... at 5 pegs to a block and 8 trenches just ....

I saw .... tracks this morning ... it was the same family ... which raided me that ... scared the pigeons yesterday .. they sneak about in the rocks .. above.

I can't see them but the ... birds .... out of a fi ... tree that grows .... gave his lubra the checkered blanket as it was too heavy for me to carry and useless at this time of the year ... black fellow wears white band in his hair and he has a white haired ... so anyone may know him.

I'm now going to try the 80 mile dash to Mt. Olga ... will travel all .... is nearly .... Till we meet again ... all be well ....

Harry.

... then there is a photo of a water hole, it is on the West Australian border. I had a swim in it .... lovely, it is 150 feet long and 22 feet wide over half its length and over six feet deep at the other end which ... to 15 feet. I'm sorry .... the diary I kept of .... last trip of mine, it ... should have had interested ... headquarters Towny ... across central Australia ... and ......

Blacks tried to kill me today while I was waiting .... three spears were thrown but two shots drove them off one spear landed in the tree that I had my back against within three inches of my neck the other two were on the side – they have smoked in the whole tribe I saw three big smokes – a lot of blacks moving for the camp .... will make fo ... and thence to the .... and may reach .... These blacks seem ...... and gave me a rabbit they he ... so I gave them my remaining blanket .... one old fellow took a fancy to my hat, which was falling to pieces, so I gave it .. him .... have tied my head .... a .... point out the camel pad to the ... young men and told them they could have all they could ...

They seemed to unders ... a good deal and I tried .... them so send a message by .... smoke signals to Alice Spgs.

Darling I've pegged the reef and marked the exact locality on the map which is buried in my kit on the sandhill where the camels bolted – on the East side .... of hill and I photographed the datum .... peg dated 23 Dec ... can't understand .... relief .... 28 acre .... 5 pegs to a block and 8 trenches just ...

... he had 15 men and 2 spears each bar my path to a rabbit burrow up ...... creek I took a risk and unloaded my revolver ostentatiously I had only 3 live cartridges in it anyway, then folded my arms and walked right up and thr' the cordon, then went and camped at his campfire body touching body and slept the night thr' ....

... figure out the amount of work ... there would be 120 .. a mov ... work for .... men.

I made myself some rabbit .. sor .. dear you would laugh at me in them, but they are easy on my feet.

I buried 3 rolls of film in a 5 lb. treacle tin on the sandhill too, there are some interesting photos ...

RENE DARLING,

Don't grieve for me. I've done my best and have pegged the reef, not strictly according to law as the blacks pinched my miners right and I don't know the number but I photographed the datum post on the Quartz Blow the post is sticking in the water hole and the photo faces north. I made the run in 5 days but the blacks have a sacred place nearby and will pull the peg up for sure.

I've taken the films and will plant them at Winter's Glen if I can get there the Blight has got me beat.

Take good care of Bobby, Betty, and Joy please, I want Bobby to be a Civil Engineer try and educate him for that.

Darling I do love you so I'm sorry I can't be with you at the last but God's will be done.

Yours ever,
x Harry x x x

... engaged to go with the camels that if I did not turn up again by the .. of November tha th ... would send a man .... Johannsen to my relief. As I believe he also stumbled on this identical reef I had to go right out to Lake Christopher which is 100 miles across the W.A. border in order to get me .. bearings then I was g ... to go direct to the reef. The company was .... soften the tale of my sufferings here. If I could only know what the trouble is all about that no relief was sent or anything done at all. Oh it is awful indeed and the skeleton of me can scarce support the weight of my clothes. I'm an awful sight and the flies are maddening and ants something that Hell can not improve on.

The blacks must have seen me burying stuff on the sandhill for they brought in the films that I had buried under the fire so I have now buried them under the floor of cave top end. I scratched the hole out last night when I felt sure they were not about. But oh what does it matter I want relief and have saved one cartridge but will stick it out as long as possible. The old man has just come and pointed the water and bough shelter out to me again saying "capei caro" "capei caro" about one dozen times.

I am giving him this book and saying: "Alice Springs," "Alice Springs," 100 times.

Kindest regards to all dear and kiss mother for me.

I loved you always as I love you now with all my heart and soul.

Old fellow returned with despatch book today having failed to get thro' to Alice Springs. He was all played out so I gave him a rabbit I had dug out .... two old men dropped in and said something to him and he turned into a block of wood for density. I wonder if the old men knew I was trying to educate him and objected. Poisoned. Today I crept out to try and get some green feed and chewed a herb which was poison. Old man with wart very kind young blacks gathered around and laughed fired my 3 shots and they ran like hell paroxysms passed but too weak to move.

Love Harry.

Later in the day the black who had first raided my camp showed up and told the tribe that I had tried to shoot him.

I had only turned in about an hour when 20 of them came down, woke me up and told me they were going to kill me, the headman who is so treacherous being the leader and spokesman. I succeeded in bluffing them by talking a lot and refusing to get up. I told them ... and they postponed the killing till tomorrow ..... (he heard me yell "I'll shoot") ..... as soon as I was assured they had retired I rose and made a moonlight flit for five miles back to the cave again (the old fellow had moved my camp for me to where rabbits were more plentiful) now that tomorrow is here and they find I have moved I expect an attack in force tonight. In the dust of the cave I have just unearthed an unexpected find 5 revolver cartridges tho' as they know I am practically blind that may not avail me much. Two or more spears were carried by each man. No doubt they were in deadly earnest too. So I don't suppose I've an earthly chance of surviving. I can carry 2 gallons and 3 pints of water but that is hardly likely to take me the 80 miles to Mt. Olga and on no food whatever. I've brought this all on myself by going alone but I thought the blacks, tho' primitive, were fair dealing. Good Bye and God Bless you Rene darling wife of mine and may God bless the children.

Harry.

..... it is now 25 days since the camels bolted – allowing 10 days to Ilbilba they should be near home by now, then people will speculate a week as to where I am then someone will be sent to Ilbilba a black probably who will loiter on the way – then too late camels will be ...... despatched over my route 360 miles via Ilbilba and a motor truck could get to me in two days if they ....

Give my love to the children and may we meet again.

Darling I have always believed in a God, a super ruler of the universe, but I have gone my own way so long that I'm ashamed to pray to Him now.

I know "call upon me in the time of trouble and I will deliver thee", but my ideas of time of .... and His may not come. I have taken up 10 holes in my waist belt and still it is loose so you can see how I have fallen away. I'm just a skeleton now and I always thou .... of the black till now, only 2 weeks ago or less I made them some beautiful .... now they are waiting for me to die in order to steal my shirt and trousers off the body.

I suppose the children have grown immensely since I saw them last, Joy may not remember me but the others will. How I would love to see them once more, to romp on the ... with them and to have their chubby arms around me.

Of course I was a fool to take on alone but relied on Paul Johns to overtake me in 4 to 6 weeks at the outside. He averred that he would overtake me in three weeks and gave his word of Honor not to let me .....

Also it was agreed upon .... Fred Blakely when I ......

Here I am established with plenty of water but no food ... even then I might have won out on 3 lbs rice were it not for the sandy blight blinding me 'till I was unable to .... follow tracks.

I suppose the plans I buried under camp fire are blistered .... and .... with heat I ought to have buried them in this cave .....

This agony is awful 4 plums in ...... three days ... no relief .... what became of Paul .... suspense of .... not knowing ... I expected .... relief .... following me .....

I erred in treating the natives too .... kindly Paul was right in saying you .... must treat them rough.

I am paying the penalty with my life. May this be a lesson to others.

DEAR RENE,

I think I am near my finish I am nearl .... and crazy with sandy blig .... tormented with flies and ants. As a last resource I soused my eyes in Lourdes Water last night and they are much clearer today .... so weak from .... back of .... can hardly walk of .... crous .... cartridges .... shoot.

I have shrunk from 35 to 29 inches and my waist line has an even greater shrinkage. I don't know wheth .. to record it as a miracle or .... but my eyes seem a lot easier since I soused them with Lourdes Water yesterday and that night I was able to get a rabbit ......

.... last night .. unpleasant surprise .... party 20 strong came down suddenly .... woke me .... told me .. were going to kill me for saying I would shoot a blackfellow .. told me to get up and be speared .... *Currotta* whatever that word means they were .. deadly earnest ......

... I flatly refused to get up ...... postponed the killing again till today. I see my finish as soon as they .... raise the rest of the tribe to rush the cave .. they can stand on top and spear me as soon as I come near the entrance anyway ... unexpected find .. 5 revolver cartridges .... hope I can make every shot tell. The chief ..... previously mentioned .... leader .... party. ....

Darling I want you to remember me as when we first met and not the scarecrow that I now am. Have shrunk still further and the flies and ants have nearly eaten my face away. I can do nothing against them "beaten by Sandy Blight" what an epitaph ...

I don't know for sure what happened to Paul Johns but I left him within reach of civilization and he understood and could talk the language fluently .... I've tried to amuse the blacks by drawing pictures but somehow they don't appeal. I am as helpless as a kitten now and they know it. I was turned adrift this morning and told to shift for myself ....

I have watched and hoped for relief till I am about the end of my tether ....
with lots of water I can hold out for several days yet but agony of
starvation may drive me to shoot myself.

I think it is the worst possible death with one experience of this
country I should never have gone alone but I relied on Paul to follow me
what good a reef worth millions I would give it all for a loaf of bread and
to think that only a week away is lots of tucker the blacks are not
troubling me now they know I'm dying and will wait ......

Good Bye Rene darling wife mine and don't grieve remember you
must live for the children now dear, but it does seem cruel to die alone out
here because I have been always good to blacks.

–my last prayer is "God be merciful to me as a sinner and be good to
those I leave behind."

x x x Harry x

Lasseter's Diary dug up in the cave.

31. FRAGMENTS

Taylor's letter of Instruction to Robert Buck – being the letter sent in by Lasseter per Paul Johns to the Company, giving instructions as to how he could be tracked and followed. [This letter of instruction was not inserted in the earlier editions of this book, as Mr. E. H. Bailey, the Secretary of the Company, asked me to withhold it pending the result of the second expedition.]

I hereby give you particulars of the work I wish you to carry out on behalf of my company.

I wish you to proceed with all possible haste to the gap at Bowley's Range, between the River Shaw and Irvine Creek and look for a lone hill upon which you will see a single tree; on this hill you will find the remains of a camp fire in the ashes of which you may find a tin containing a letter of instruction. Failing to find anything there go north to Sandstone Rock Reservoir and look for a letter there; should you again find nothing return to the gap at Bowley's Range and go to Mt. Curdie and on to McBain's Springs and Henry Hull Spring, all the time looking for tracks and letters in old camp fires – at the same time asking any natives you may meet if they have seen a white man with two camels, the white man, being short and stumpy in build. You will at this point cross the border into W.A. and on to Giles Pinnacle, Sladen Waters, along the Rawlinson Range to Lake Christopher. At this lake look either in the centre one of three fires which are reported to be kept burning there. Or look for a hill named Centre Mount Fire, situated on the Lake: should you discover nothing spend a reasonable amount of time searching the neighbourhood for tracks, etc. and should you be unsuccessful return without delay, but make quite sure that Lasseter is not about before you return.

I am leaving an agreement for you to put your signature to, I trust that it will be to your satisfaction, Rev. Albrecht will send it on to me with your name attached.

I am leaving an agreement for you to put your signature and you will find all your saddles in good order.

Wishing you the best success in your trip. I am,

Yours faithfully,

P. Taylor.

For the C.A.G.E. Co., Ltd.

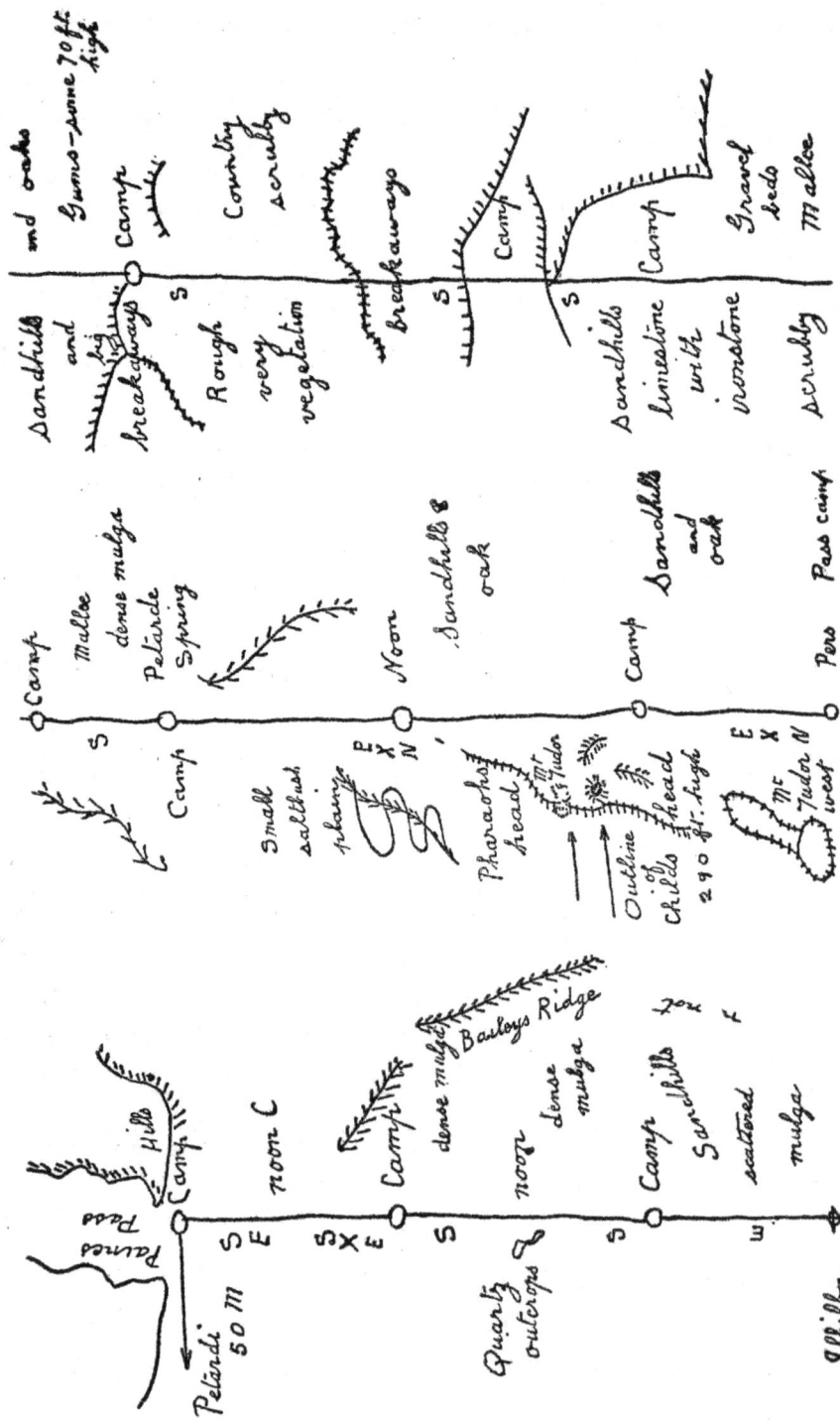

Sandhills and big breakaways

Gums—some 70 ft. high and oaks

Camp

Rough very vegetation

Country scrubby

S

breakaways

Camp

S

Sandhills limestone with ironstone

Camp

S

Gravel beds

Mallee

scrubby

Camp

Mallee dense mulga

Pelarde Spring

Camp

S

Small saltbush plains

E X N

Sandhills & oak

Noon

Pharaoh's head

Mt Tudor

Outline of Childs head 290 ft. high

Camp

Sandhills and oak

E X N

Mt Tudor west

Pero

Pass camp

Pelardi 50 M

Paines Pass

Camp

Hills

S E

noon C

S X E

Quartz outcrops

Baileys Ridge

dense mulga

S

Camp

noon

dense mulga

S

Camp

Sandhills for scattered mulga

W

Illbilba

Ayers Rock

E
X
S   Mt Olga

Sandhills & mulga

S

Breakaways

Diffault country

Near lake gums and
Scattered mulga   oak

Lake Amadeus

Bob Knob

3

Sandhills

Camp o desert oaks
Glilba S Patches of big gums

Sandhills   cutting out

Limestone country

Scale 1 ——— 17mile (estimated on plans)

Junifer   Mr Rennie Bearing N 8W

Mulga

Sc d   Mallee getting dense

Mulga

Can go   back now

Area   L. n t x d ground
fine
sto
g.go slow

9

Sa th c

Spring 4

o Small o nobs

Camp
Plain

Mulga

Sc th d gums

gum swamp

cho.
Scattered. thro
sandhills

Robert Buck set out with his own team of camels and natives. The result of this search has been told in earlier chapters of the book.

Again we come to the diary found by members of the second expedition.

The following reproduction of part of the sketch-plan of the route followed by Lasseter was easily decipherable in the red notebook portion of his diary. Some of the leaves, however, are missing.

The last three pages of the sketch-plan here reproduced (marked Fragments of sketch in rolled-up diary) are just indecipherable. There are fragments of other sheets with traces of pencil marks, faint directions, and indecipherable portions of words here and there.

Where and what do these fragments lead to?

These sketches mark the partial finish of a remarkable story of courage, faith and dogged perseverance to the last. The story proves that "Truth is stranger than fiction." The days of romance and thrilling adventure are with us still.

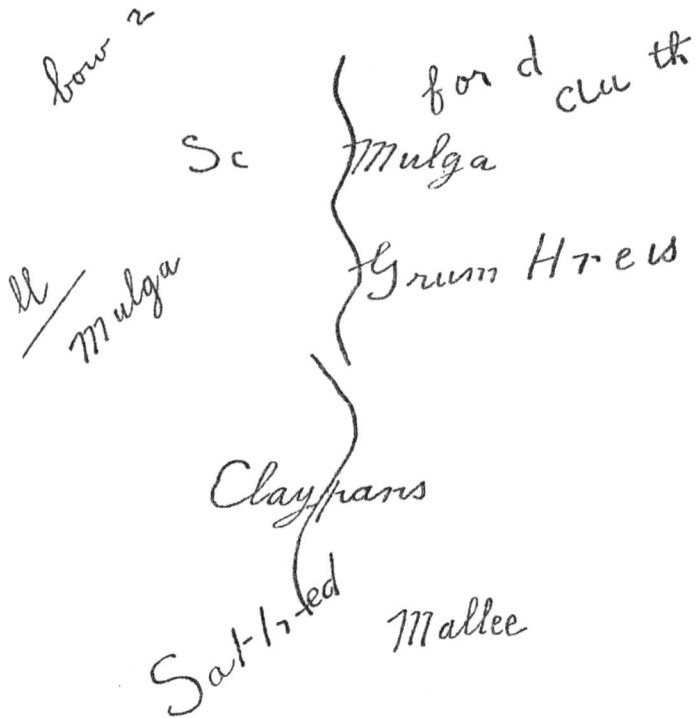

So ended the attempt of a particularly determined man to open up that big area of new land which has defied many. Twelve men already have given their lives in the attempt to cross its distances and solve the question of its mineral wealth. But these and similar pioneers did not die in vain. By such deeds Australia was opened up; others inevitably follow in the steps of the pathfinders. This big unknown area towards the west of the Centre will eventually be crossed from north to south and east to west, and thoroughly explored, for new country calls to every man.

And we breed the men to answer the call.

PROSPECTING FOR GOLD

ION IDRIESS

From the Dish to the Hydraulic Plant, and from the Dolly to the Stamper Battery. With chapters on Prospecting for Opal, Tin, and other Minerals; and a chapter on Prospecting for Oil, by Dr W. G. Woolnough, F.G.S., Geologist to the Commonwealth of Australia. Illustrated.

This book, written by a prospector with a lifetime's experience, will save the new chum gold-seeker much labour and time and disappointment, and will teach the old hand many a payable wrinkle.

Dr W. G. Woolnough (Geologist to the Commonwealth of Australia) :-"Your hints should be invaluable to all, beginners and experienced men alike."

Canadian Mining and Metallurgical Bulletin:-"The volume will arouse the reader's interest at the outset and hold it to the end."

Queensland Government Mining Journal :-"It tersely sums up a lifetime's knowledge gained at first hand acquired by a man well equipped to pass his experience on to others."

Engineering and Mining Journal (New York) :-"This book is replete with good methods, described simply. Lack of space forbids quoting the terse directions."

Rabaul Times (New Guinea) :-"Invaluable. Each bit of advice and information is practical, as it comes from an old-time miner himself."

Now in its 20th edition, 190 pages, available from ETT Imprint.

LASSETER'S DIARY

Transcribed with Mud-Maps

Harold Bell Lasseter had always claimed he had found an immense reef of gold hundreds of miles west of Alice Springs. In 1930, with Australia in the grip of Depression, a privately funded expedition led by Fred Blakeley, accompanied Lasseter in an attempt to relocate the reef. Blakeley left Lasseter at Ililba, and Lasseter continued his trek towards the Olgas with a dingo shooter and their camels. Lasseter continued to be introspective and brood, prompting Lasseter to go off alone with two camels.

In March 1931 an expedition led by bushman Bob Buck found Lasseter's body at Winter's Glen, and his diary at Hull's Creek, wherein it describes how after his camels bolted, he was alone in the desert, encountering a group of nomadic Aboriginals who offered offer him food and shelter. Blind, exhausted and dying, Lasseter made one last attempt to walk from Hull's Creek to Uluru.

The diary was purchased by Ion Idriess from Lasseter's widow in 1931, and from it he wrote the best-seller Lasseter's Last Ride. Tom Thompson has transcribed the diary with its original mud-maps, including those not in the diary itself and Lasseter's drawings.

First edition, 90 pages, available from ETT Imprint.

THE DESERT COLUMN
An Australian Trooper in Gallipoli and Palestine

ION IDRIESS

With a Foreword by General Sir Harry Chauvel, G.C.M.G., K.C.B., late Commanding the Desert Mounted Corps.

Scotsman (Edinburgh) :-"His book, valuable as a document of war, is an absorbing example of descriptive reporting .... Difficulties and dangers, escapades and escapes, fill the pages of the book with excitement."

W. Farmer Whyte in the *Daily Mail* (Brisbane) :-"In *The Desert Column*, which has brought the author letters from over half the globe, we have a War Diary which, for its stark realism and colourful descriptions, has certainly not been surpassed."

Natal Mercury (South Africa) :-"One of the most vivid pieces of war narrative that has ever been written .... "

Cavalry Journal (London) :-"Personality, accuracy, and a fine spirit breathe through its pages. It can be heartily recommended to all cavalry readers."

Montreal Daily Star (Canada) :-"The author is a born writer, and he has missed nothing of the drama, the comedy, the tragedy, and the intense humanity of the scene."

New Zealand Magazine:-"His book is a perfect thing in its way .... It is as animated and realistic as a cinematograph film. *The Desert Column* deserves shelf room in every New Zealand home."

Now in its 26th edition, 272 pages, available from ETT Imprint.

THE YELLOW JOSS

ION IDRIESS

With Foreword by Tony Grey. Illustrated.

Sydney Morning Herald :-"The Booya is a masterpiece of the weird and terrible. But of all the tales "The Castaway" has most power and surely merits a place with similar episodes in Conrad. Mr Idriess is adept in working up the feelings of his readers to a pitch of expectancy .... Here the excitement is terrific."

The Herald (Melbourne) :-"Every one of these tales bears the impress of truth. Anybody who lets unreasoned prejudice against short stories deter them from reading this book is missing a treat."

The Sun (Sydney) :-"Idriess tells a good story. These come from another world, a primitive and violent world, where things that seem fantastic and incredible to dwellers in the Australian cities are commonplaces of life."

Queensland Times :-"He has the happy knack of being able to blend truth and fiction in such a way that even commonplace things assume an important role and have definite and impelling force."

Woman's Budget (Sydney) :-"They give a clearer insight into his varied and adventurous life than anything he has previously written."

Honi Soit (University of Sydney) :-"Rich humour enlivens the book, particularly where the exploits of one 'Scandalous' Graham are concerned."

Producers' Review (Brisbane) :-"The name of Ion Idriess has become a household word ... as a maker of short stories he has lost none of his flair for tale-telling. Indeed we prefer this style."

Now in its 10th edition, 190 pages, available from ETT Imprint.

DRUMS OF MER

ION IDRIESS

With Foreword by Wm H. MacFarlane, Mission Priest, Torres Strait Administrator of the Diocese of Carpentaria.

Professor T. G. Tucker, Litt.D. (Camb.), Hon. Litt.D. (Dublin), writes :-"Apart from his evident knowledge of the natives and their customs, Idriess has a graphic power greater than that of any writer whom I have read for years. His accounts of a battle of canoes, the wreck of a flotilla, and other events, are the finest things of the kind that anyone out here has produced."

Christchurch Times (N.Z.) :-"Idriess's Masterpiece. To enter into the life of a savage race of a bygone age, and to make that life spring into renewed reality, so that the blood runs hot and cold in response to its splendour and its degrada¬tion-this is" the feat, almost an unparalleled feat, that has been achieved by Ion Idriess in *Drums of Mer* .... Idriess must now rank as the most brilliant star in the literary galaxy of Australia, and world fame for him can only be a question of time."

Sydney Mail :-"In dramatic appeal it is superior to *Gold-Dust and Ashes* and *The Desert Column* ... that should be sufficient."

Pacific Islands Monthly:-"Mr Idriess, in the telling of his story, displays sheer genius. There is something here for the scientist, the historian, the geographer, the beauty lover, and the student of the occult. *Drums of Mer* is not only a story, it is an invaluable addition to the historical records of the Pacific Islands."

The Argus (Melbourne) :-"He has seized upon the most colourful aspects of this decayed civilization before it has been completely lost to living memory, and has dramatized them with his uncanny gift for realistic narrative writing."

Now in its 23th edition, 260 pages, available from ETT Imprint.

I ON IDRIESS

'Jack' Idriess was born in 1891 and served in the 5th Light Horse in the First World War. He returned to Australia to write The Desert Column, which was published following his huge success with Prospecting for Gold. He went on to write 56 books and was largely responsible for popularising Australian writing at a time when local publishing was still not considered viable. A small wiry mild-mannered man, Idriess was a wanderer and adventurer, with a vast pride in Australia, past, present and future.

ETT IMPRINT has been publishing Idriess for over 25 years, including:

Flynn of the Inland
The Desert Column
The Red Chief
Nemarluk
Horrie the Wog Dog
Prospecting for Gold
Drums of Mer
Madman's Island
The Yellow Joss
Forty Fathoms Deep
Lasseter's Last Ride
The Cattle King (audio)
Sniping
Shoot to Kill
Guerrilla Tactics
The Wild White Man of Badu
Gold Dust and Ashes
Headhunters of the Coral Sea

www.ingramcontent.com/pod-product-compliance
Lightning Source LLC
Chambersburg PA
CBHW030935090426